The MGA, MGB and MGC

The MGA, MGB and MGC

A collector's guide

by Graham Robson

MOTOR RACING PUBLICATIONS LTD
28 Devonshire Road, Chiswick, London W4 2HD, England

First published 1978
Second Edition 1982
Reprinted 1984
ISBN 0 900549 73 4

Photosetting by Zee Creative Ltd., London SE19
Printed in Great Britain by The Garden City Press Ltd.,
Letchworth, Hertfordshire

Contents

An aerial view of the Abingdon factory, taken from the north. The buildings in the centre foreground are not part of the factory itself, but are part of the original Pavlova works. The main assembly lines are in the block towards the top centre in this shot, and ancillary operations are carried out in the block to the right. In the 1960s the famous Competitions Department was housed at the far end of that block, and the holy of holies, the design and development departments, were at the end nearest the camera. Since this picture was taken the large area between all the buildings has become a massive parking/dispatch area for new cars. The new Special Tuning block now stands where cars are closely packed together on the extreme right. Abingdon town is off to the left (actually to the east), and the Abingdon bypass now cuts across country to the far right of this picture.

Introduction

Every other sports car manufacturer in the world must be jealous of MG. Probably no-one else can match a tradition going back more than 50 years, a sporting reputation which has rarely flagged, and a following which is huge. The MG is arguably the world's best-known and best-loved sports car. It is also much the most prolific — and that is incontestable fact; without even a nod to the romance of sports car motoring and reputations, the sales figures can speak for themselves.

By the beginning of 1978 nearly 1.3 million MGs of all types had been built, more than 800,000 of these being sporting two-seaters. At its peak, Abingdon can turn out more than 50,000 cars a year — which means that the entire pre-war total of MG production (1924 to 1939) can be surpassed in five months!

Even so, all over the world people are buying MGs — new and not-so-new — with little idea as to a car's design and development history. Because Leyland Cars have had to drop active service and technical support to older models there are thousands of owners who keep their cars going by inspiration and perspiration, but against a background of ignorance.

It would be quite impossible to sort out every MG in one book; better authors than myself have tried, and failed. Because they are much the most numerous, and because they are the models still in goodly supply at reasonable prices, I have decided to concentrate on the more modern MGs, starting with the MGA of 1955.

This, then, is a book mainly of facts. I hope it will make clear the way in which the first 'BMC-based' MG sports car was developed, how it became better, faster, and more exciting, and how eventually it was replaced by a much-improved car in 1962, which is still in production and selling well. In the 23 years since the MGA appeared there have been many changes and improvements to these MG sports cars, and I hope the significant ones are all listed here. Which MGs could have automatic transmission? Which have an all-synchromesh gearbox? How have the United States 'federal' regulations affected the car? What are the secrets of the near-mythical MGA 1600 De Luxe? How closely-related is an MGC to an Austin-Healey 3000? Was the MGB V8 a success or a failure, and why? When did disc brakes arrive? Reclining seats? Radial-ply tyres? Who built the bodies? What about five-bearing engines? All this, and more, has been analysed.

I hope I have also been able to sort out the works competition cars, and more particularly some of the intriguing prototypes which had an important bearing on the MGAs and MGBs you could buy. Among those you *couldn't* buy were UMG 400 (the Le Mans TD), EX 214 (the Frua-bodied MGA), EX 234 (the Farina-styled MGB replacement) and ADO 21 (a mid-engined car designed at the end of the 1960s). Who knows what might even be in the works for 1979 and beyond?

Leyland Cars have generously provided almost all the photographs, and I am very grateful for them. They have also beavered away for hours to help me complete the factual and statistical Appendices, which will probably be as interesting to many historians and MG-watchers as the rest of the book. Which models were successes and which, relatively speaking, were failures? The sales figures tell us much more than any road test or press release can possibly provide.

But I must make one thing crystal-clear. This book is neither a reminiscence nor a requiem. The MGB is selling very well, almost as well in 1978 as in any previous year, and in North America it has established its own tradition. Euphoric company salesmen are already talking about a Beetle-like phenomenon for the car. According to current forecasts, the half-millionth MGB should roll off the production lines in 1979, and the millionth Abingdon-manufactured car should follow by the end of that year. As the least fashionable of all the factories controlled by British Leyland, Abingdon is surely the jewel in their crown?

GRAHAM ROBSON

May 1978

Introduction to Second Edition

To re-read the original introduction to this book is to realize how quickly things change at Abingdon. By the end of 1979 the Midget had been dropped and the MG was isolated at Abingdon, eventually to be joined by the Vanden Plas Princess 1500. During 1980 it became clear that the MGB's days were numbered, and the last MGB of all was built in the autumn. The factory has since been sold by BL (and mostly demolished), the MG name went into temporary cold storage and has re-emerged on a high-performance Metro saloon. Eventually, about 513,000 MGBs were to be built before the closure, and this Second Edition wraps up their story to its rather bitter and disillusioned end.

GRAHAM ROBSON

June 1982

Acknowledgements

No-one could tackle a book like this without help, advice and expertise from the real experts. So I'd like to say a big 'Thank You' to the following:

From British Leyland: Tony Barson, John Cooper, Barry Crook, John Davenport, Ian Elliott, John Harvey, Don Hayter, Peter Hazael, Peter Hutton, John McLellan, Terry Mitchell, Bill Price, Peter Sharp, Mick Woodley, Anders Clausager.

From the MG clubs: Roche Bentley, Gordon Cobban, John Hill, Colin Light, Derek and Pearl McGlen, Phil Richer.

From the magazines: Warren Allport, Michael Bowler, Lionel Burrell, Ray Hutton, Susan Jones.

For personal research: Geoffrey Healey and Richard Langworth.

I owe a special note of gratitude to British Leyland for supplying all but a handful of the illustrations. A few other illustrations were provided by *Autocar* (pages 45, 53, 92 and 107), and the prototype Austin-Healey 3000 Coupe picture is by Pininfarina.

GRAHAM ROBSON

CHAPTER 1

Ancestors and parentage

YA, TD and TF

Without stretching the point too far, I could claim that the MGA of 1955 was really the first post-war MG sports car, but that needs some explanation. In the first 10 post-war years, of course, there were three successful MG two-seater series, but they all had close and definite links with MGs designed in the 1930s. The TC was only a lightly modified 1939 TB, while the TD and TF shared the same chassis, developed from that of the YA saloon, which had been designed in 1938 and 1939. The MGA, apart from its front suspension, had no mechanical links with older designs, and is truly the first of the modern MGs.

In the beginning the MG was the brainchild of Cecil Kimber, who was manager of Morris Garages in Oxford, a company owned by the redoubtable William Morris, whose 'bullnose' cars were already making a name for themselves. The first MGs were modified Morris cars, built in 1923-24 (when the first car with an MG badge was actually delivered is still a matter of conjecture) and assembled in Oxford.

Sales expanded steadily, and the final move to Abingdon (to a factory once used by the Pavlova Leather Company) was made in 1929. The first MG Midgets, a line for which MG is still rightly famous, was announced in the autumn of 1928, and its successful racing career got under way with a vengeance in 1930 when the 'Tomato Growers' took the Team Prize in the Brooklands 'Double Twelve'-hour race.

Until 1935 Midgets grew faster, more powerful and technically more sophisticated. At the same time Cecil Kimber pursued an active motor racing programme, whose success gave the MG marque's reputation a great boost. This was all well and good for the sporting enthusiast, but Morris (who had now become Lord Nuffield) was not one of them. Kimber's policy gave rise to fine cars, but it did nothing for MG's profits. In 1935 Lord Nuffield sold his own (personally-owned) MG company to the Nuffield Group. The new owners immediately closed down the racing operation, closed down the Abingdon design office, and set about making MG cars profitably.

For the next 20 years MG's fortunes were directed from Nuffield headquarters at Cowley, though Kimber remained as managing director until the early years of the war. Between 1936 and 1939 MG's new models were the TA, TB, VA, SA and WA, all being closely based on Morris and Wolseley mechanical parts.

When the Second World War broke out in September 1939, the group had been almost ready to launch a new MG saloon car — the YA — which was destined not to meet its public until 1947. This is an important link in the design chain which led to the MGA in 1955.

I must delve back even further. In the autumn of 1938 Morris had launched the Series E Morris 8, and by then Alec Issigonis and Gerald Palmer were working away at Cowley on an MG version of the car, which would have a new chassis with independent front suspension, and the 1,250cc engine (in detuned form) which was already slated for the TB. This new car, therefore, was a rather ramshackle mixture of Morris 8, Morris 10 and MG parts, which emerged in a most homogenous form as the MG YA in 1947.

Although the YA family (there was a short-lived YT tourer and an improved YB saloon to follow the YA) was only a qualified success, which sold 7,413 examples, it was an important progenitor of the TD and TF sports cars. The TC two-seater, of

The YA saloon, introduced in 1947, was probably the true ancestor of all modern MGs. Based on the four-door bodyshell of the 1938 Morris 8 Series E model, it was designed in 1938 and 1939, and but for the outbreak of war would probably have been a new MG model for 1940. In the event its introduction was delayed for seven years, but it was sold in its original design form. Although the car was basically a Morris Motors design, it was assembled at Abingdon. The YA was succeeded by the improved YB saloon, and there was also an export-orientated YT tourer.

This is the rolling chassis of the MG YA saloon introduced in 1947. Its links with more modern MGs are that it had a sturdy box-section frame, it used a single-carburettor version of the XPAG 1,250cc engine, and it was the first MG production car to have independent front suspension. Note, however, that the frame is underslung at the rear — in other words the main frame side-members pass under the back axle, which restricts that component's rebound movement.

By comparing this TD/TF chassis with that of the MG YA it is possible to see the common parentage. For the sports cars the wheelbase was reduced by five inches to 7ft 10in and the side-members were swept up and over the line of the back axle. The engine, of course, was in a higher state of tune (originally it was nearly identical to that of the TC) and a remote-control gear extension was fitted. Note the Nuffield-type hypoid back axle. The sturdy steel tube situated just ahead of the steering wheel was used to stiffen up the body and eliminate scuttle shake, and to provide a measure of roll-over protection.

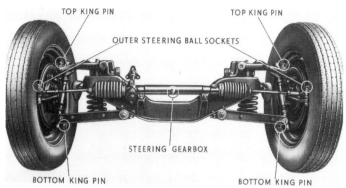

The independent front suspension used on YA/YB, TD/TF and subsequently on MGA production cars was designed by Alec Issigonis in 1938. Forty years later, in considerably modified and developed form, the MGB layout was still based on this design, and only the MGC (which used longitudinal torsion bars and telescopic dampers) has used a basically different arrangement.

The original MG TD of 1950 used steel disc wheels (without any perforations or other decoration) and predictably this caused a great deal of controversy among MG enthusiasts. The body design was still traditionally styled, and construction was of steel panelling on an ash frame.

which 10,000 were built between 1945 and 1949, was a 1930s design, with a flexible ladder-type chassis, and stiff half-elliptic leaf springs at front and rear. When the time came for a successor to be developed, it took only a few days for a YA chassis to be chopped about, and for a modified TC body to be dropped on to it.

That was in 1949, and the Cowley design office refined the idea in time for the TD's launch at the beginning of 1950. The definitive TD chassis was rather different from that of the YA saloon in that its box-section side-members were swept up and over the line of the rear axle (instead of running under it). But if the chassis was more modern the TD's looks were still traditional. Even so, 29,664 TDs would be sold before the end of production in 1953.

We now begin to see the first glimmering indication of an all-new MG shape, the one which would eventually mature as the famous and well-loved MGA. Although MG's design work had been carried out at Cowley since 1935, a small nucleus of design and development engineers worked on at Abingdon, among them Syd Enever and Alec Hounslow, and even the anti-racing Nuffield management turned a blind eye when they interested themselves in MG record-breakers, and cars being prepared for production sports and saloon car races.

A bluff and burly *Autosport* photographer, George Phillips, now joins the story. Phillips was a motor racing enthusiast, and competed in the Le Mans 24 Hours race in 1949 and 1950 with his own MG TC specials. For 1951, with better aerodynamics (and a higher top speed) in mind, MG agreed to design and build a new open bodyshell to mate with an MG TD chassis for the ebullient Phillips to use at Le Mans.

This car, registered UMG 400, was styled empirically by Syd Enever, and had unmistakable lines not copied from any other car. The only problem was that the driver sat on, rather than in, a TD's chassis, such that Phillips was more exposed to the air stream than would otherwise have been ideal. In those days, of course, the semi-reclining driving position had never been tried.

UMG 400 was obviously based on the TD chassis (the road wheels were a clear giveaway) and had a rather high bonnet line to clear the tall XPAG engine's tappet cover. It was undoubtedly an effective shape, for in the race it achieved a 116 mph maximum speed and lapped consistently at more than 80 mph. It achieved

Later MG TDs — generally called TD II models — had perforated wheels and slightly more engine power, but wire wheels were never offered.

The MG TF, introduced in 1953 and destined to be built for less than two years, was to be the last of the traditionally-shaped MG sports cars. Compared with the TD it had a more shapely tail and fuel tank, but under the skin the chassis frame was virtually unaltered.

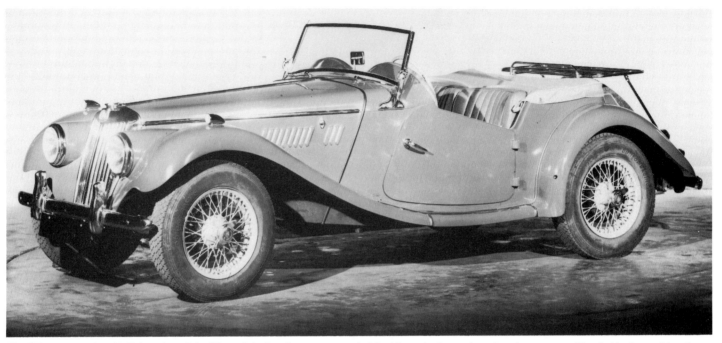

The TF's nose was less bluff than that of the TD, and the headlamps were partly faired-in to the front wings, but the car was still styled in the traditional way. Note, however, that centre-lock wire wheels had been reintroduced as optional extras.

no lasting fame, as the normally-reliable XPAG engine dropped a valve after only two hours' racing.

Even though there was no official development budget to cover his next move, Syd Enever was so irritated by the special's poor driving position that he decided to design a proper chassis frame to suit the new body. Rumour has it that this was laid out in the traditional manner — on a dining room table — and the fact is that by the beginning of 1952 a couple of frames had been constructed. These were swept much wider in the scuttle area that the TD's frame had been, which allowed the seats to be dropped considerably. They were also very strong, with massive scuttle-bracing superstructures made of box-section steel members.

One frame formed the basis of a new experimental MG, given

the Abingdon code number of EX175, on to which a slightly revised version of the special Le Mans body was mated. This, however, was completely trimmed and finished, with bumpers, windscreen, hood and sidescreens. However, although this car was *a* prototype of the next all-new MG, it was not *the* prototype. EX175, registered HMO 6, and affectionately known by that name for years, used a 1,250cc XPAG engine, a TD gearbox and the TD's hypoid-bevel back axle. It was, however, nearer to the real thing than UMG 400 had been, principally because the Phillips Le Mans special was built on an obsolete chassis frame.

Enever and John Thornley (MG's newly-appointed general manager) were both convinced that they had a new product which could take over from the TD as soon as management would

14

Close-up of the TF's independent front suspension, not at all hidden by the front wings. The dual function of the lever-arm shock absorbers, the mounting of the rack-and-pinion steering and the positioning of the conical bump rubber are all obvious. Bumpers, which were standard fittings on the TF, had been removed for this picture to be taken.

The TF's facia, complete with octagon-shaped instrument bezels, of which Cecil Kimber would surely have approved! There was no change to this instrument layout, whether or not the cars were equipped with left-hand or right-hand steering. Note the tiny roller-type accelerator pedal.

approve it, and hastened to show it to their masters. The problem was that since the beginning of 1952 MG had become a part of the BMC group (which combined Nuffield with Austin); although Lord Nuffield was still the company's chairman, the man who made all the active decisions was Leonard Lord, of Austin.

Enever and Thornley got to Len Lord just three days too late. During 1952 Lord had let it be known that he might support a sports car design built to use Austin parts (especially the hard-to-sell A90 power trains), and this had attracted interest from Jensen, Frazer Nash — and Healey. Donald Healey's new 100 model was so startlingly pretty that Lord took it under Austin's wing straight away, and rejected everything else.

MG could not even point to declining demand for their existing car — the TD — as they sold 10,838 of them (more than the entire output of TCs in five years) in 1952 alone. Lord directed that EX175 should be put away as it was not needed at that time.

History now tells us that demand for TDs began to flag almost from that time. Both Austin-Healey and Triumph (with their TR2) helped signal the change in sports car fashions, but Len Lord would not see it. He authorized only a major TD facelift, which was carried out in 1953 and was shown later that year as the TF. But it was too late. At its best the TF sold only half as well as the TD had done, and even uprating it with the 1,466cc XPEG engine couldn't save the situation. In June 1954 BMC made two important decisions — EX175 got the go-ahead and the full Abingdon design office was reopened.

It was an exciting and bustling time for Abingdon. They were back in business with a vengeance, they had a new project to get ready for production, they were also building MG Magnette and Riley saloons, and the famous MG Competitions Department was being reopened under the management of Marcus Chambers.

Compared with 1935, however, there was one important difference. Then they had effectively been their own masters. Now, in spite of a brave show to the contrary, they were being controlled fairly closely from Longbridge and Cowley. The new car would have to comply with corporate policy (such as it was), and would have to use corporate components. MG traditions, and MG dedication, however, made sure that it was still an exciting product. 1955 was probably the most critical year which MG had ever had to face.

Evolution towards a modern style. This new shape for an MG sports car was proposed by Nuffield chief designer Gerald Palmer in 1953, even before the TF had been launched. His view was that while there was controversy over styling it should be possible to offer two different styles on the same chassis. Using the TD/TF chassis and running gear (he had not, at that point, been instructed to consider the use of Austin components), he suggested that this could be the 'modern' style. Although it was not unduly modern, it had one advantage — all the skin panels were bolt-on items attached to a common body base which could also accept traditional panelling...

...as exemplified by the alternative style, shown here. Different wings and doors could have been bolted on to the basic structure. This ingenious scheme was rejected, and the designs never progressed beyond the mock-up stage. These pictures were taken in the Nuffield Group's styling studios at Cowley, which have long since been closed down.

The genesis of the legendary MGA was a special bodyshell produced at Abingdon for a racing TD which George Phillips proposed to race at Le Mans in 1951. Its only real disadvantage, caused by the fact that the seats had to sit on the chassis frame rather than be slung down inside the main side-members, was that the driver sat rather high. Alec Hounslow is at the wheel, with Syd Enever (in the suit) alongside him and the mechanics responsible for building the car grouped round the car. The tiny bonnet scoop was to ram cold air into the race-tuned TD XPAG engine.

A plumb side view of George Phillips' TD shows that compared with the later MGA the crown-line of the front wing dropped more abruptly as it passed along the doors, which were therefore considerably shallower, while the rear wings were smaller. The front grille and apron were also different, the headlamps were closer to the ground, and there was no left-side door. Syd Enever is at the wheel.

Almost there! This is the famous EX175 prototype, registered HMO 6 and built in 1952 for approval by Len Lord as MG's successor to the TD. As such it had a new chassis-frame, later used for the MGA, but it used the TD engine, gearbox and back axle. This explains the bonnet hump, which was needed to give clearance over the XPAG engine's rocker cover. Apart from this detail, and the fact that the windscreen was slightly shallower than the finalized design, the body shape was carried over completely in the MGA production car. Work on this car, however, was suspended in 1952 when Len Lord chose the Healey — later the Austin-Healey — 100 for production, and the TF was developed in a hurry instead. When EX175 was revived in June 1954 it had to be re-engineered with B-Series BMC mechanicals. Like UMG 400, HMO 6 has not survived.

CHAPTER 2

MGA and MGA Twin-Cam

1955 to 1962

Work went ahead rapidly on the new car, and each part was released for production tooling to be made as soon as it could be cleared from the drawing office. The original plan was that the new car, on which work had started in June 1954, should be in production from April 1955, and that worldwide announcement could be made at the beginning of June 1955. This would have been a wonderful way to launch the new car, as the Le Mans race for which a team of cars was to be entered (see Chapter 3) was to be held at the same time, but unfortunately the production schedules could not be met due to a delay in the supply of production bodyshells.

The new car, soon to be named MGA, was coded EX182, and while visually and structurally similar to EX175 it was radically different under the skin. Whereas the massively strong chassis frame (later experience suggested that it was, if anything, *too* strong) and the bodyshell were virtually as schemed out in 1952, and the TD/TF wishbone front suspension was to be retained, the entire power train was new.

This was because BMC had embarked on an aggressive policy of rationalization, which was already becoming apparent to the public. In their scheme of things there was no future for Nuffield-based items like the TD/TF engine, nor its transmission and rear axle. Instead, MG were instructed to use a tuned version of the Austin-designed 1,489cc B-Series engine (which would not begin to be replaced until 1978), along with the new B-Series gearbox and rear axle. These had already found a home in a modern MG, the ZA Magnette saloon, which had been designed at Cowley by Gerald Palmer in 1950-51 and was now being assembled at Abingdon. It must be said in his defence that he had laid out the

Magnette (along with the related Wolseley 4/44) to take the TD/TF power train; the Austin-Nuffield merger of 1952 had come too late to stop the Wolseley keeping its version of the MG power train, but the MG Magnette had had to be redesigned at Len Lord's insistence.

Working back along the power train, therefore, the MGA would have a three-bearing 1,489cc engine in tuned form, which in one form or another was already being used in BMC cars like the Austin A40, the Morris Oxford, the MG Magnette, and even in BMC vans. The gearbox case had been designed for steering-column control in mass-produced Austin and Morris cars, but had already been skilfully converted to floor-change operation for use in the MG Magnette. The MGA installation was the same as that of the Magnette except that a further gear-change extension was added to the B-Series case to allow the lever to be placed even further back in the cockpit of the new sports car. Theoretically this made the gear-change linkage long and potentially floppy, but as any MGA enthusiast will know an assembly in good condition provides delightfully direct control. The box itself had side-mounted selector forks and a side rather than a top cover; it would be used on MGs up to 1967, after which the all-new all-synchromesh Mk II MGB box would take its place.

The axle itself was a three-quarter-floating hypoid-bevel unit with a banjo-style housing, also to be found on the newly-announced Austin/Morris/MG cars (and soon to be seen on Riley and Wolseley models as well). Subject to a small reduction in track, the axle and brakes were common with the components fitted to the Magnette saloon. It is interesting to recall that at the time the car was being developed John Thornley thought the

The production MGA was revealed, at last, in September 1955. In its general shape it was similar to the Le Mans cars which had already been seen in public, and it was a complete contrast with any previous MG sports car. Its chassis and power train were new from end to end with the single and important exception of the front suspension, which had been carried over from the TD/TF series. In standard form there were hinged flaps in the side curtains for the passengers to extend their arms to make signals or rude gestures. The MGA, like the TF before it (but not the original TD) had flashing direction indicators.

The clean lines of the original MGA 1500 shown in the Cowley styling studios. The petrol filler cap is hidden behind the offside tail-lamp, and this is a typical home-market car fitted with the optional radio. Centre-lock wire wheels were optional extras. There were no external door handles; the doors had to be opened by pull cables inside the doors, reached by inserting a hand through the side-curtain flap. The car, therefore, was not at all thief-proof.

centre-lock wire-wheel option, while essential for marketing purposes, would only be a passing fashion, and that centre-lock disc wheels would soon take over. At the end of the 1970s, however, wire wheels were still to be with us, and still very popular!

For the MGA the axle ratio would be 4.3:1, whereas the other models with this axle used 4.875 and 5.125 ratios. This axle was to have a very long life in MG cars, and would only be made obsolete on the MGB by the Salisbury-type axle first introduced on the MGB GT in 1965 and on the MGB Tourer from 1967. For certain Leyland Austin-Morris models this basic axle was still in production in 1978.

There was, therefore, virtually no carry over of any important items from the TF. Only the front suspension and steering, and the very best of MG's traditions, remained. The new car was designed to be made in very large quantities, but no-one could have known how well the MGA would succeed. The TC's best year (1948) had seen 3,085 cars produced, while the TD's peak of 10,838 (1952) had set an all-time record for any MG. The MGA was to shatter that record in its first full year, and in both 1957 and 1959 more than 20,000 examples would leave Abingdon between January and December.

With this sort of production in mind, the two most complex components — the bodyshell and the chassis frame — were bought out. The chassis frames were pressed by John Thompson, Motor Pressing, Ltd, of Wolverhampton, but welded-up at Abingdon. Bodyshells were welded-up from steel and light-alloy pressings at the Morris Bodies Branch in Coventry (which had once been a Riley factory in pre-rationalization days), painted and trimmed at this factory, then dispatched to Abingdon by transporter lorries for final assembly. The door skins, the bonnet panel and the boot lid were all panelled in aluminium alloy, the rest of the shell being of pressed steel. Not for many years had an MG sports car body been completely built outside Abingdon, but this, after all, was the first MG shell to be made entirely from pressed-steel parts, welded together, a process which needs a lot of space and a great deal of heavy (and costly) equipment.

When the new car was announced in September 1955 it came as no great surprise to MG enthusiasts. They had, after all, seen the trio of EX182 prototypes race at Le Mans in June, and again in the Tourist Trophy in September (these events are detailed in

Not much room in the boot of an MGA as the spare wheel took up a good deal of the available space, which in any case was rather shallow. Completely equipped production cars had a flexible cover over the spare wheel, and the tool roll lived in the same space. The boot-lid had to be propped open by a long rod, as shown here.

Chapter 3), and no attempt had been made to disguise their significance to MG's future. MG TF production ran out in the spring of 1955, well before production of the MGA could begin, and it was only the assembly of MG Magnette and RM-series Riley saloons which kept Abingdon ticking over in the summer of 1955.

The new car had a distinctive shape, but while clearly related to both UMG 400 and HMO 6, it was slightly different from both. Comparing the cars, George Phillips' Le Mans TD is seen as having a more pronounced dip in the crown line of the front wing and door top, and rather less shaping to the rear wings. The tail of the production car was subtly more smooth in several areas, with a bigger boot lid and different tail lamps. The two grilles, too, were obviously different, and the production car needed no scoop in the bonnet panel to channel cold air to the engine bay. The

The MGA's facia, as first produced in 1955; apart from very minor changes to instruments, this would remain virtually unaltered throughout the life of the model. Features were sensible and easily-read instruments — the all-important rev-counter being ahead of the driver's eyes instead of centrally-placed as in the TF — a central horn button which could be worked by either occupant, a built-in grille behind which the radio loudspeaker could be installed and a map light for the passenger. The whole layout was 'handed', in other words instruments changed sides when left-hand drive was fitted.

MGA, on the other hand, had decorative hot-air outlets on each side of the bonnet opening, where UMG 400 had had none at all. The production car needed no bonnet bulge to clear the top of its engine, and the line ahead of the driver's eyes was very smooth. A major and obvious difference in layout was that the production car had its fuel tank under the boot floor, with the filler cap near the offside tail lamp, while Phillips' car had a snap-action cap immediately behind the driver's head, and a tank above the back axle.

The 1,489cc engine, in production form, while not as powerful as those used at Le Mans, was still the most lusty yet shown by BMC from their B-Series design. In basic layout it was a very conventional three-bearing engine, with its camshaft, pushrods, ports and manifolding all concentrated on one side (the near side) of the unit, and all the 'hang-on' electrical items, including starter, dynamo and distributor, on the other side. The cylinder-head was not the same as that used at Le Mans; like all production

derivatives of this engine (all of which were made on the same transfer machinery at Longbridge), it had heart-shaped combustion-chamber profiles and — inescapably because of the layout of the valve gear — siamesed inlet ports *and* a central siamesed exhaust port collecting spent gases from the middle two cylinders. Carburation was by two semi-downdraught 1½-in SU units, and there was a nicely-shaped cast-iron exhaust manifold linking to a single-tube exhaust pipe.

It is worth noting several traditional MG features which were in the design, including the lever-arm dampers at front and rear (the front dampers also doubled their duties by forming part of the front suspension's wishbone layout), the fitting of two six-volt batteries, wired in series and tucked in to the floor behind the seats, the simple build-it-yourself hood, and fixed plastic side-screens incorporating a flap to allow hand signals and provide access to the door latch from the outside. The MGA, like the TF, had flashing direction indicators — the TD, when announced in

The massive and cleverly laid-out MGA chassis, with widely-swept side-members which allowed the seats to be dropped well down. Two six-volt batteries lived in the floor area ahead of the back axle, but behind the seats, while the big (10 gallon) fuel tank was placed low down at the rear between the chassis side-members. Note that the fly-off handbrake was tucked in to one side of the tunnel, ideally positioned for the driver to grab it in a competition manoeuvre.

1950, of course, had not had indicators of any kind.

The facia, too, was a welcome return to tradition and sanity. In developing the TF, almost in a desperate attempt to keep the T-series design alive as it were, the designers had given the car a garish instrument board with octagonal dial surrounds which were not even ahead of the driver's eyes. MGA dials, however, were sensible and circular, with the rev-counter and speedometer placed behind the steering wheel, one each side of the steering column. The fly-off handbrake was to the side of the tunnel (the TD/TF brake had been on top of the tunnel), but was still very effective, and the gear-change was both precise and ideally placed. A radio was optional, as was the fresh-air heater (the TF had had an optional recirculating heater). The MGA could be ordered with steel disc or centre-lock wire wheels, and other worthwhile

extras included a 4.55:1 axle ratio, a telescopic steering column and a tonneau cover. At first there was no optional hardtop, but this would follow in a year's time.

When released the car was placarded with 68 bhp at 5,500 rpm, but this figure was speedily improved to 72 bhp, and almost all MGA 1500s built have this improved rating. It is interesting to note that the MG Magnette saloon of its day had a very similar engine rated at 60 bhp at 4,600 rpm. Both of these outputs, incidentally, should be compared with the 82.5 bhp claimed for the Le Mans cars raced in 1955.

With a full range of colours on offer, with production beginning ahead of announcement and with sales beginning at once, the MGA was a sure-fire success. It might not have been as fast as either the Triumph TR2/TR3 (the TR3 was announced at

The TF-type independent front suspension was carried over unchanged to the MGA, as was the rack-and-pinion steering, which fitted most unobtrusively into the nose of the chassis-frame area.

all?) was soon forgotten. If it had any drawbacks at all it was that it always looked faster than it actually was — a real tribute to Syd Enever's inspired body shape.

After only a year, the open sports car was joined by the very smart and practical MGA Coupe. This should in no way be confused with any MGA supplied with a detachable hardtop, as it was a completely different concept. Copying, in a way, the Jaguar XK success story, MG staff decided that they could also sell a version of the MGA with a permanently fixed roof and many saloon-type refinements. The MGA Coupe, therefore, was given a pressed-steel roof, allied to a new and unique semi-wraparound windscreen and a wraparound rear window. The doors were altered to incorporate wind-up glass windows, and were fitted

The MGA 1500 production engine (rated first at 68 bhp but soon uprated to 72 bhp) was a modification of the standardized BMC B-Series unit. For MG the carburation (twin 1½ in SUs), manifolding, camshaft profile and internal details were special, though they had much in common with the engines fitted to the Nuffield-designed MG Magnette saloons. The capacity was 1,489cc, as indicated by the figure '1500' cast into the wall of the cylinder-block. The gearbox casing is not complete in this view, neither are the extension and gear-lever linkage fitted. 'Mowog', incidentally, was a BMC spare-parts trademark.

the same 1955 Motor Show) or the Austin-Healey 100, but it could usually nudge 100 mph in favourable conditions (*The Autocar* test recorded a mean maximum speed of 98 mph), and it was undeniably very good value. Its original British-market price was £595 (this rose to £640 in May 1956), which compared with £550 for the obsolete MG TF, £650 for the TR3, and £750 for the Austin-Healey 100. Exotica like the Jaguar XK140 were priced right out of reach at £1,217.

Just over 1,000 MGAs were built before the end of 1955, but in 1956 cars were leaving the gates at the rate of nearly 300 a week. It was no wonder that Riley production ceased in the summer of 1955 to make way for the new flood of MG sports cars — until 1957 only MGs were built at Abingdon, at which juncture production of Austin-Healey 100/6s began, and it would not be until 1960 that a new non-sporting product (the Morris Minor van, no less!) would again intrude on the scene.

Right away the MGA was a great success. It was faster, smoother and more civilized than the TF had been, it was enormously strong, and the presence of non-MG engines (but had the TD/TF unit *really* been all that special to Abingdon, after

The optional detachable hardtop was available on MGAs from 1956, along with sliding sidescreens; these allowed them to be used as snug little closed cars and — important in sporting circles — to run as Grand Touring cars in races and rallies. The detachable top became a very popular extra over the years, and many private-enterprise tops were also on offer.

with very neat exterior handles which fitted flush to the door frame when not in operation.

The Coupe was introduced at £699 at a time when the Tourer cost £640; it was mechanically identical to the Tourer, but was unavoidably a little heavier, in fact about 100 lb heavier at first. Although it received a good share of publicity at the time of its launch, thereafter it was somewhat neglected. Yet the Coupe remained in production until the end of the MGA's run in 1962, which means that there are examples of all models, including the Twin-Cams and the even rarer 1600 De Luxe models, in this shape.

Introduced at about the same time, and of equal importance, especially in sporting events where a sports car with a hardtop could sometimes run as a Grand Touring car, where the competition was not as fierce, was the detachable glass-fibre hardtop option, which was supplied along with a set of rigid plastic side windows incorporating sliding screens. These much-improved sidescreens were not offered as a matter of course on the MGA without a hardtop until the 1600 model appeared, but were a great improvement in every way. This hardtop option, incidentally, should not be mistaken for the wide and confusing choice of proprietary tops for the MGA, some of which were on the market before MG were ready to start selling their own.

Thus established, the MGA sold very strongly, and was altered only in tiny details. Its price rose to £663 in May 1957 (the Coupe price rose to £724 at the same time), and at this point the suspension settings were generally tightened up a little. In these inflationary days we may not believe it, but this was the last price rise suffered by the MGA, which continued for the next five years, through two significant model improvements, at the same price level.

Time and progress now began to catch up with the MGA. Experience in competition proved that the car was a little bit too heavy (that phenomenally sturdy chassis frame was partly to blame) and slightly underpowered compared with some of its opposition. Furthermore, the enormous success of the disc-braked Triumph TR3 had brought new standards in braking to this type of car. The combined effect of these influences brought about the MGA 1600 model, which was phased into production in the summer of 1959.

There was no need to change the basic concept of the car, and there were in fact no changes of note to the suspension, steering, transmission and general fittings. To commonize with the cylinder block of the MGA Twin-Cam (which I describe at the end of this chapter) the engine was enlarged to 1,588cc, with an increased cylinder bore. At the same time rotating parts were strengthened, lead-indium big-end bearings were adopted and the power output was increased to 79.5 bhp at 5,600 rpm. The big change, however, was to the brakes, for MG adopted Lockheed 11-in diameter discs for the front wheels, these being matched to the existing 10-in diameter rear drum brakes. Visually, the only style changes were to standardize sliding side-screens and to use

The original MGA's engine room, showing the modified BMC B-Series engine. I have always found the wiring and plumbing arrangements to be untidy, but there is no doubt that access for maintenance is good, if not as good as that offered by a traditional MG with fold-up bonnet panel sides.

amber-coloured front flasher lenses, along with completely separate lenses at the rear for flashing indicators and tail lamps. The MGA now became a genuine 100 mph car, with acceleration to match. The all-up weight had crept up very slightly, and average fuel consumption figures fell because most owners took full advantage of the extra performance.

MGA sales were given an immediate boost. In 1958, 16,122 cars had been sold. In 1959, the year in which the MGA 1600 was announced, 7,644 of the old model were delivered, and a further 14,156 1600s followed; the grand total for the year (Twin-Cams included) was 23,319. It was the best figure ever for this model, and this from a crowded Abingdon now also frantically trying to satisfy orders for the Austin-Healey 3000s and the little Austin-Healey Sprites (which had gone on sale in the summer of 1958).

There was one corporate problem, however, namely that the MGA's 1,588cc engine size was a complete oddity. Not then, nor at any time later, would a BMC saloon car have this engine size, which was fine for MGAs to contest the up-to-1,600cc competition classes, but very bad news for production planners who had to alter the tools every time a batch of MGA cylinder-blocks had to be machined.

It really came as no surprise, therefore, when we learned that the MGA 1600 (restrospectively known as the Mk I, though never badged as such, nor labelled as such in BMC literature) had been discontinued from April 1961. In its place came the final version of the car, the model rejoicing in the long-winded title of MGA 1600 Mk II. In total, 31,501 1600 Mk Is were built, only 415 of them in 1961, by which time Mk II production was rapidly building up.

The Mk II, at least, is instantly recognizable at a casual glance. From the front, its modified radiator grille is obvious. The vertical bars have the same spatial position at the top of the main surround, but sweep down almost vertically to be housed well back from the front lower lip of the surround. As one cynic remarked when he saw the car: 'Oh good, I see it's had its accident without any attention from the owners . . .'

At the rear yet another type of tail lamp was fitted. Gone was the raised plinth on the wings, and gone were the two separate lamp lenses. In their place was a single horizontal strip lens, incorporating stop, tail and flashing-indicator functions. The Mk II's other appearance revisions were confined to detail, like the

The smart and nicely-trimmed MGA Coupe was announced in the autumn of 1956. Almost all the open bodyshell was used, but the doors were considerably changed, with wind-up window glasses, and the Coupe top was of pressed-steel, welded to the rest of the shell on assembly at the Morris Bodies Branch in Coventry. Although it never received a great deal of publicity the Coupe remained in production, with whatever engines were current, until the MGA was dropped in the summer of 1962. As evidenced by the model girl's clothes, this is a contemporary picture, taken in the autumn of 1956.

Although wire wheels were an option on the Coupe, this car has the perforated disc wheels which were standard equipment.

27

The neat and tidy method of providing exterior door handles for the MGA Coupe, which was both practical and safe. When not being operated, the door handle lay snugly against the pillar. The doors not only had wind-up windows, but also swivelling quarter windows.

limit for competition purposes, and it was only done by a far-reaching change to the engine's layout.

A completely revised cylinder-block was needed, with new cores and with pairs of cylinders siamesed. A new cylinder-head casting was used, with improved porting and air-flow possibilities, along with larger (by 0.063-in) inlet valves. The combustion chamber was reshaped and enlarged, so to maintain a high (8.9:1) compression ratio the new pistons had flat tops instead of concave crowns. The increased capacity was gained merely by increasing the cylinder bore from 75.4 mm to 76.2 mm (throughout the life of the B-Series engine the 88.9 mm stroke was never to be changed); the resulting capacity of 1,622cc may seem strange until it is realized that bore and stroke dimensions in good old Imperial measure were now 3.0 x 3.5-in!

The result of all these changes was that the new engine's power output rose to 86 bhp (net) at 5,500 rpm, with a torque boost to match. For the first and only time on a push-rod MGA it was possible to raise the gearing, with a new back-axle ratio of 4.1:1.

Unfortunately, time was now running out for the MGA. When the 1600 Mk II was revealed in June 1961 (in the same week, by clever publicity, as the first of the Sprite-based Midgets was shown) the basic body style had been on public view for six years, and people who had already bought perhaps two or three MGAs were beginning to wonder if they should bother buying something which continued to look just the same.

The designers, too, had the monocoque MGB up their sleeves and nearing the production stage, so it is hardly surprising that the Mk II was only on sale for 15 months, in production for about the same time and that it only sold to the tune of 8,719 examples. Even so, it was with great pride that the 100,000th MGA, a 1600 Mk II, was completed at Abingdon in March 1962 — an achievement then unmatched by any other true sports car in the world (Triumph's combined TR2/TR3/TR3A total couldn't get near this, even though the car was in production for at least as long) and in certain events the 1600 Mk II was still competitive to the end of its life.

In seven years, therefore, the developing design stayed commendably and triumphantly unchanged in concept, which made (and still does make) the search for spare parts that much easier. Although there is a great deal of difference between the three basic engine designs of 1,489, 1,588 and 1,622cc, which is

covering of the facia and scuttle top with matt plastic material to cut reflections (in previous open MGAs they had been painted metal).

The big change, however, was to the engine. Although for the time being the Mk II would have a completely unique BMC B-Series engine size, all the other bread-and-butter BMC models would fall into line with it in October 1961. Although the increase in capacity — from 1,588cc to 1,622cc — was only 34cc, this was enough to move the MGA firmly out of the 1,600cc class

This side-view of an MGA Coupe shows off the sleek lines of the metal top, and one needs little persuasion to see that this variant on the MGA theme was even more aerodynamically 'clean' than the original Tourer. Both screen and rear window were considerably bowed, not for any esoteric reasons of fashion, but because that gave the correct combination of looks and good aerodynamics.

No changes to the rear of the MGA Coupe compared with the open car, but there were strengthening ribs down each side of the rear window, which would not have been rigid enough if built in one piece. On MGAs, the rear number plate was always free-standing like this, with the number-plate lamp above it.

The rare and excitingly-fast MGA Twin-Cam model was announced in 1958, though the engine itself had already been seen in racing MGAs and in purpose-built MG record cars on many occasions. By the time all the auxiliaries and accessories had been packed in with the bulky new Twin-Cam engine some routine servicing was not at all straightforward. In this view, for example, it is quite impossible to see the distributor, which is tucked away in the nose under the water hose from the radiator to the remote water header tank, while the oil filter is completely hidden under the carburettors and shrouded by bodywork. The Twin-Cam was a little heavier than the equivalent pushrod ohv-engined MGA, but this did not affect the roadholding or the balance of handling.

by no means confined to simple considerations of pistons and other details, but includes major items like crankshafts, cylinder-blocks, cylinder-heads and allied parts, the rest of the transmission, all the suspension and the entire structure was virtually common throughout.

Total production, between start-up in summer 1955 and shutdown in July 1962, was 98,970 cars with pushrod ohv engines. The majority of these cars were sold overseas, and the greatest number of all was sold in the United States.

It is time, now, to turn to the intriguing MGA Twin-Cam model, which by almost any standards existing at Abingdon, must be counted as a commercial failure. In less than two years of production, (the car was withdrawn abruptly at the beginning of 1960) only 2,111 examples were sold. At its best, in 1959, only 80 cars a week were being built.

The Twin-Cam was a twinkle in Cowley designer Gerald Palmer's eye as early as 1954; using the basis of the B-Series engine as his building-block, he schemed a twin-overhead-camshaft conversion for sports car use, and handed it over to the proper design office — the Morris Engines Branch at Coventry — to be detailed and developed. As explained in the next chapter, the engine was first seen in public in September 1955, when the MGA Le Mans car LBL 301 used a prototype engine in the Tourist Trophy race at the Dundrod circuit in Northern Ireland.

Development took a good deal of time, and it was not until the summer of 1958 (after further-developed engines had been used in the EX179 and EX181 record cars in 1956 and 1957, respectively) that the production-built units were ready. These, though based on the standard B-Series cylinder-block and bottom end, as Gerald Palmer had always intended, were nevertheless almost entirely special. The cylinder-block itself, for instance, was bored out from 73.025 mm to 75.4 mm, the water jacket cores were revised to make allowances for this, and the finish-machining processes were carried out at the Morris Engines factory in Coventry.

Heavily domed pistons were used on a new design of connecting-rod, giving a very high compression ratio of 9.9:1, which meant that the engine had to run on the very best 5-star petrol to give of its best. The special light-alloy cylinder-head, with twin overhead camshafts, Jaguar/Coventry Climax-style valve operation by inverted bucket-type tappets, and an included angle of 80 degrees between the valve alignments, was entirely machined at Coventry. The camshafts and the relocated distributor were driven by a combination of gear and duplex chain drives, all hidden by a complex new front casting. A big, finned, cast sump pan, an impressive exhaust manifold and twin semi-downdraught 1¾-in SU carburettors complete the picture of a very bulky unit which really filled the MGA's engine bay. The carburettors, incidentally, had swopped sides compared with those of the pushrod engine; on the Twin-Cam the carburettors

are to the off-side (or right-hand side). This relocation of carburettors made the moving of the distributor essential.

As launched the engine displaced 1,588cc and produced a most impressive 108 bhp (net) at 6,700 rpm. Because the engine merely revved harder, and continued to breathe when the pushrod engine was beginning to over-rev, there was no change to the gearing, nor to the gearbox itself.

The Twin-Cam's chassis was also almost the same as that of the

The exhaust side of the Twin-Cam engine looked brutally efficient and purposeful. The basic cast-iron cylinder-block was sandwiched between a light-alloy cylinder-head and an alloy oil sump, and the front of the unit was dominated by a complex timing cover which incorporated a new position for the distributor drive. There was a separate cast header tank, seen here resting above the cast-iron exhaust-manifold pipes. The dipstick is the long tube leading down to the tail of the sump, near the flywheel face of the cylinder-block. The usual '1600' capacity figure was cast into the cylinder-block, but this is obscured in this picture by the engine mounting plate.

The production Twin-Cam engine, built in 1,588cc form for a full year before the pushrod ohv engine was enlarged from 1,489cc to the same capacity, was based on the pushrod engine's cylinder block, but was otherwise almost completely new. Major new castings like the cylinder-head and the sump are obvious, but even the cylinder-block was modified so that there was no distributor drive, nor a dipstick and dipstick access on this side of the engine. Starter motor (not in place in this engine shot), dynamo, oil filter and other details, however, were in their familiar positions.

MGA 1500, except in detail. There was an important development to brakes and wheels, but apart from this the most important difference was that the mounting for the steering rack was an inch further forward (so that clearance with the more bulky engine was maintained at a satisfactory level) and the steering arms were lengthened to suit; this, incidentally, had the effect of making the steering slightly less responsive. Spring rates were raised slightly to compensate for the heavier engine, and

A head-on shot of the Twin-Cam engine emphasizes how wide it had become compared with the usual pushrod ohv engine. Inside the complex cast front cover is the primary gear drive from the crankshaft to the jackshaft (in the old pushrod engine's camshaft tunnel, but now reduced to driving the repositioned distributor, the oil pump and the rev-counter), and the twin camshafts are driven by a single duplex roller chain from the jackshaft. The cooling fan (not fitted, incidentally, on the original racing engines) is driven off the water pump spindle. The included angle between the two lines of valves is 80 degrees, symmetrically disposed about the cylinder centre-line. As laid-out originally by Gerald Palmer and detailed by Morris Engines it had a 90 degree angle, but this was reduced during the development period. The A & M designation on the front cover refers to company which supplied the castings for machining.

there were other minor suspension structural changes to make the car more robust.

The big news apart from the engine was that the MGA Twin-Cam was fitted with four-wheel Dunlop disc brakes, and that it was sold with centre-lock Dunlop disc wheels, without the option of wire wheels. Four-wheel discs had been proven on cars like the Jensen 541s and (in greater quantities) on the Jaguar XK150s and 2.4/3.4 saloon car models. Their only real drawback was that it was difficult to provide efficient hand-brake systems. There was no vacuum servo in this MG installation, but the sensitivity was perfectly acceptable for all that.

Twin-Cam chassis identification is complex, and needs explanation:

Y indicates a Twin-Cam car
D indicates a Tourer
M indicates a Coupe
1 indicates a RHD Home-market car
2 indicates a RHD Export-market car
3 indicates a LHD model
H5 indicates an Export CKD model

This gives such typical combinations as YD1, YM2, or YD3, with other permutations, followed by a chassis number between 501 and 2611. There were just 133 CKD cars exported in kits, mainly to South Africa.

Yet despite all the changes, and a very exciting performance, the MGA Twin-Cam was a commercial failure. Why? It can be summed up in three succinct words — cost, reliability and the TR3A. I'm sorry to drag in the question of an opposing model, but it happens to be very important in this case.

In Britain, the Twin-Cam sold for £843 basic (the Coupe version cost £904), at a time when the TR3A sold for £699 and the Austin-Healey 100/6 (also built at Abingdon) for £817. This would not have been a great problem if the Twin-Cam could offer significantly better performance than these two cars, but the Austin-Healey was quicker in all respects, and the TR3A was faster at least up to about 80 mph, more economical and much more simple.

The biggest problem was one of reliability, and the irony was that MG had come to terms with the problems, and cured them, just before it was decided to withdraw the model. The very high compression ratio meant that the engine had to have its spark

Externally, the only recognition points of an MGA Twin-Cam were the road wheels and the badges behind the ventilation holes on each side of the bonnet panel. No changes were needed to the radiator grille to ensure an adequate flow of cooling air to the radiator and the engine bay.

Compared with the pushrod MGA 1500, the Twin-Cam's facia and cockpit were only slightly changed. Vinyl covered the main panel and there were extra controls, but the general layout was identical. The rev-counter and speedometer markings were the main giveaway, with the rev-counter yellow sector starting at 6,500rpm and calibrations extending to 7,500rpm, and the speedometer markings extended to 120mph. When the 1600 was revealed in 1959 the differences would be even less obvious.

timing absolutely right and had to use the very best fuel; if either was significantly away from the optimum piston burning was almost certain to occur. This, in conjunction with a propensity for burning oil on early models due to the combination of chromed piston rings and chrome molybdenum treatment for the cylinder-bores on the first 345 engines, soon led to the Twin-Cam getting a bad name.

As with the later MGC, however, there is no doubt that this was case of 'giving a dog a bad name', as a good Twin-Cam could be very good indeed. But with demand for the pushrod models booming as never before, and with corporate policy favouring the 3-litre-engined Austin-Healey 3000, it was decided to discontinue the Twin-Cam. Arch-enthusiast Mike Ellman-Brown took delivery of the very last example during 1960, and still owns it

with pride.

To deal with the engine's combustion problem, the compression ratio was dropped from 9.9 to 8.3:1 by the use of different pistons, and this became effective from Chassis Number 2251 in the summer of 1959. All engines, when rebuilt by BMC, were given these low-compression pistons, and there is no doubt that reliability was much improved at only a minor cost in power output and performance. That the engines were, with development, both strong and potentially very powerful, was proved by such competition cars as the Ted Lund Twin-Cam and the two cars campaigned so successfully by the Dick Jacobs team.

It is worth noting that detachable access panels were fitted to inner wheelarches from Chassis Number 592, and that the MGA 1600 decorative changes were phased-in at Chassis Number 2192.

A front anti-roll bar was standardized from Chassis Number 2275.

The Twin-Cam, of course, is well-known, but the resulting derivative of it, using a normal pushrod engine, is much less familiar. A car never truly recognized as a separate model in the MGA line-up (as recently reaffirmed to me by spares and service executives within Leyland) was the De Luxe version of both MGA 1600 and MGA 1600 Mk II cars.

These cars, to all intents and purposes, were really Twin-Cams

The centre-lock pressed-steel road wheels standardized for the MGA Twin-Cam. 5.90-section Dunlop RS4 Roadspeed tyres were also standard (compared with 5.60-section tyres on the pushrod-engined cars). The Twin-Cam's suspension, braking and wheel/tyre specification was also available for the unpublicised MGA 1600 De Luxe models, and regularly found its way on to works competition cars of that period.

fitted with the appropriate pushrod ohv engine. This is to say that the entire Twin-Cam chassis items (centre-lock disc wheels, different steering layout and suspension details, along with the four-wheel Dunlop disc brakes) were allied to the normal pushrod 1,588cc or 1,622cc MGA engines.

That much is no mystery; the mystery was that, for many years, no-one at MG or any other part of British Leyland appeared to know how many of these cars were built, nor how much they cost (they were never officially price-listed). Certainly no service-support literature was ever issued to back up their preservation.

Behind the smokescreen, undoubtedly, was the need to get a very desirable derivative homologated for competitions, which meant that the authorities had to be convinced that more than 500 cars of any particular type had been constructed. Indeed, although De Luxe models began to be made in June 1960, immediately after the Twin-Cam had been discontinued, there was no obvious attempt to publicize their existence until the 1600 died away. When the Mk II was announced in June 1961, *The Autocar* commented: 'Dunlop disc brakes front and rear, in conjunction with centre-lock wire wheels, are also obtainable . . .' The reference to wire wheels is a mistake in this context, but the inference is clear. It was one way of letting people know that Twin-Cam items could still be supplied, and it confirms that not all De Luxe models were as completely equipped as others.

The Twin-Cam items were very valuable for use on works-team pushrod MGAs. They found favour in several cars built for use in the Sebring 12 Hours race, and they also helped to make that last-of-all MGA rally car, 151 ABL, a really formidable machine.

We know that 395 De Luxes were made in all — 82 1600s and 313 1600 Mk IIs — of which a mere 12 were 1600 Coupes and 23 were Mk II Coupes. Strangely, no fewer than 152 cars were built towards the end, in April and May 1962.

Between 1955 and 1962, the total number of MGAs of all types built was 101,081, and unless a car was involved in a very terminal accident you may be sure that its sturdy chassis frame will have survived the last two decades. When Syd Enever laid out that frame in 1952 he probably erred just a little on the side of strength and durability. With the new model he and his team began to develop towards the end of the 1950s he was determined to add further to the strength without adding to the weight. The long-running MGB was to be the result.

The Lockheed front disc-brake installation should be compared with the Dunlop disc brake used in the MGA Twin-Cams; it is clear that they are very different in every way. This was the production system introduced for the MGA 1600 during the summer of 1959, and in this instance is shown for a car fitted with the optional wire wheels. On all disc-brake MGAs except the Twin-Cams and 1600 De Luxe models rear-wheel drum brakes were used.

Dunlop rear disc-brakes detail of the Twin-Cam installation, which also illustrates the wheel-attachment layout for the centre-lock Dunlop disc wheels used on this model. The separate handbrake caliper, hinged to the hydraulic footbrake caliper, is visible. On this car, as with Jaguars and other models which used this particular pattern of Dunlop brake, the handbrake effectiveness was no more than adequate when everything was properly adjusted, and downright poor if neglected over a long period.

MG historian Wilson McComb (no, that isn't a deaf-aid cord linked to his ear, it is the line of the sliding sidescreen!) posing the new MGA 1600 model at the time of its public release in 1959. Although registered in Oxfordshire, this car was built to North American specification, complete with left-hand drive and white-wall tyres. Even an MG enthusiast has to look hard for MGA 1600 recognition points in this view, which are confined to '1600' badges behind the air outlets on each side of the bonnet opening, rather different side-lamp/indicator flashers and the sliding sidescreens.

General and close-up rear views of the 1959 MGA 1600 showing the revised tail-lamps and the '1600' motif below the distinctive MG octagon. The functions of the stop/tail lamp and the indicators were separated, the former being mounted lower on a new plinth with the indicator lamp above it.

The MGA 1600 engine bay, showing few important changes compared with the original 1500. Do not be misled by the original picture on page 26 as this was of a car in which the optional fresh-air heater and associated piping and trunking were not installed. For a left-hand drive car, of course, the brake and clutch master-cylinder and pedal-box assembly change sides.

The manifold-side view of the MGA 1600 engine, showing that it was virtually the same as the original 1500. However, the '1600' identification cast into the side of the cylinder-block will be noted, and the detail difference in petrol overflow pipe routing is obvious. This photograph illustrates how long and complex were the gear-selection arrangements. The short gear-lever extension was unique to the MGA (most related applications of this gearbox used a lever sprouting straight out of the tail-shaft casing (at which point the special MGA casing is bolted. The physical selection of gears is at a position in the gear casing behind the irregular-shaped patch plate fixed by ten bolts or screws to the side of the main casing.

The last variant of the MGA theme was the car with a rather long-winded name — the MGA 1600 Mk II. Once again there were no sheet-metal styling changes, but to make the nose of the car visually different from the superseded model the Mk II was given a revised grille. The bodyshell cut-out was not changed, but the grille's vertical bars were realigned into a near-vertical position. Behind the engine-bay outlets the legend '1600 Mk II' appeared. As with the 1600 press-release pictures, this is an export-market car registered in Britain.

The 1600 Mk II had a recognizable MGA facia, but minor changes included the use of a waterproof matt plastic covering of the scuttle between the base of the screen and the crash-roll; the same material was applied to the facia itself. The speedometer on this export-market car is calibrated in kilometres per hour.

The 1600 Mk II was rebadged on the tail (the same small bright-work casting was used for the bonnet and boot-lid), and new horizontal-style lamp clusters were used in which the function of tail, brake and flashing-indicator lamps was completely separated. As before, and on every MGA variant built after the end of 1956, there was a Coupe alternative. The Mk II was introduced in June 1961, at the same time as the Sprite-based MG Midget, and ran out in favour of the new MGB in July 1962.

It was a proud day in Abingdon's history, in March 1962, when the 100,000th MGA was produced. Total MGA production of all types including Twin-Cams was to be 101,081, of which only 2,111 were Twin-Cams. The 100,000 mark of pushrod cars was missed by a mere 1,030 examples. To emphasise the international nature of MG's operations at this period, the 100,000th car was built for an export market with the figure '100,000' under the usual 'MGA 1600 Mk II' script behind the engine-bay air-outlets. More than anything else, MG were proud of the fact that they had out-produced and out-sold Triumph, who had made much of the success of their TR2/TR3/TR3A cars in recent years. The trio of happy men are Syd Enever, behind the wheel of '100,000', General Manager John Thornley, with a paternal hand on the top of the screen, and a diffident-looking Cecil Cousins, MG's works manager, standing behind Enever.

CHAPTER 3

MGAs in competition

Racing and rallying, including Le Mans cars

Once BMC had given approval for the MGA project to go ahead again, there was a concerted but well-controlled rush to get the new model into production. But for most motoring enthusiasts a more immediate result of such policy changes was that they learned that John Thornley had gained approval to reopen the famous MG Competitions Department, which had meant so much to Cecil Kimber and MG in the 1930s.

Manager of the revitalized department was Marcus Chambers, who was to remain in charge until the summer of 1961. He formally took over towards the end of 1954 and had a very difficult brief. George Harriman, managing director of BMC, issued a directive which stated baldly that he wanted BMC to get to the top in motor sport, and that the necessary money to achieve this would be made available. No excuses were invited, and none would be accepted.

To get things started, and to give the new MGA model a real publicity boost, it was decided to enter a team of cars for the 1955 Le Mans 24 Hours race. This news, in itself, caused a minor sensation, for official works-prepared MGs had not raced at the Sarthe circuit since 1935 (when a team of P-Type Midgets, driven by lady drivers, had been thoroughly trounced in their capacity class by Singers), and there was considerable speculation in the motoring press as to the type of cars MG proposed to use this time. Much of this speculation, it must be admitted, was window-dressing to keep readers on tenterhooks, as quite a few journalists were privy to MG's secrets in the early months of 1955.

John Thornley's original plans were simple, and characteristically bold. He intended to be ready to announce the MGA production car during June 1955 (TF production would have tailed off by then), and he meant to publicise that launch by running three of the cars at Le Mans in the same month. This, as I have already pointed out, was foiled because the Morris Bodies Branch were not able to complete tooling for the bodyshells in time, and the production cars did not go on sale until September, three months late.

By the time this was known, however, construction of the race cars had already begun. As production cars they could have used standard pressed-steel bodyshells, but since they would now have to run as prototypes, if they were to run at all, more imaginative decisions could be made. John Thornley gained permission from the Le Mans organizers to change the cars' entry category, and while it would have been exciting to see the cars run with super-streamlined shapes, it was decided to do no more than build the shells of light alloy.

Construction of the three cars which would race — LBL 301, LBL 302 and LBL 303 — along with a spare, went ahead rapidly, and they had several interesting and special touches. The chassis and the suspension, of course, had already been successfully blooded as the basis of the 1954 EX179 record car and needed no improvement; the frame, in any case, was known to be impressively strong. But the heart of any successful competition car is its engine, and in the MGA's case this would have to be the relatively unproven BMC B-Series unit, along with its related transmission.

To make sure that it could produce an adequate power output (for performance) and to make sure that it was reliable (to last the full 24 hours) it received a lot of attention both from the BMC tuners at Abingdon and Coventry, and from the distinguished

41

A revealing test-bed shot of the first of the 1955 Le Mans MGA engines being developed. Based closely on the relatively new B-Series BMC engine, this unit was raced-tuned in a joint programme between MG, BMC, and Harry Weslake (who had become a respected air-flow consultant to BMC). From the nearside of the unit, the most obvious features were the big SU carbs (with 1¾ in chokes, compared with 1½ in on production cars) and their bell-mouth intakes. Transmission casings were mass-production items, as intended for the MGA, but a set of very-close-ratio gears were installed.

little Weslake concern in Sussex.

Based very closely on the production B-Series unit, the 'bottom end' of the engine was almost entirely standard except that lead-bronze shell bearings were used throughout. A special cast-iron cylinder-head, however, was developed for the race cars by Harry Weslake. Like the normal head it had siamesed inlet ports and a central siamesed exhaust port, but inside the casting itself the ports to the inlet valves were also carried right through to the opposite face of the cylinder-head, where they were connected by an external balance pipe. These extra 'ports' were neatly accommodated between the pairs of sparking plug positions, and were reputed to give a boost to the engine in part-throttle mid-range conditions. It would also have been possible for extra

carburettors and manifolds to be fixed to the head, but this was never done on the cars which actually raced.

The engines had no cylinder-head gaskets — a perfect seal was ensured by scraping and lapping the mating surfaces — and special pistons helped to raise the compression ratio to 9.4:1. The camshaft was special, and twin semi-downdraught 1¾-in SU carburettors were fitted. This resulted in a published output of 82.5 bhp at 6,000 rpm, with maximum torque of 85 lb ft occuring at 4,500 rpm.

A B-Series gearbox was used, complete with the unique MGA-type extension casting, but the internal ratios were very close. Compared with the production car's gears, they were:

EX182: 1.00, 1.286, 1.62, 2.45. Axle ratio 3.70

The offside of the 1955 Le Mans MG racing engine, which at a casual glance looks almost entirely standard. However, note that there is a very strange external balance pipe, bolted to the cylinder-head at two points between the end pairs of sparking plugs. The cast-iron cylinder-heads had a unique porting arrangement whereby the port passages were carried across above the valve throats. This was a Weslake invention which, if necessary, could have been developed to make the fitting of carburettors possible on *both* sides of the head! This idea was dropped before production began, when a normal B-Series cylinder-head with all the ports on the left side of the engine was adopted.

MGA prod: 1.00, 1.374, 2.214, 3.64. Axle ratio 4.30 (The axle, although of B-Series type, had a special high ratio to suit the Sarthe circuit's long straight.)

Although the bodies looked like those of the production MGA, they were mainly built of light-alloy. Naturally, no bumpers were fitted, and at the front of the car there was a fairing over the untidy recess exposed when the bumper was removed. All the light-alloy pressings, incidentally, were manufactured on the new tools, but assembly was carried out at Abingdon. There were two seats, because regulations demanded them, but a metal tonneau cover was over the passenger seat and the driver was protected only by a tiny curved screen. The boot area was almost entirely filled by a vast 20-gallon petrol tank (slung between the two

chassis side-members), and the spare wheel was positioned well forward, above the line of the axle. Policy dictated that the body should look standard; there were no compromises to this directive, such that an extra long-range driving lamp had to be partly recessed into the radiator grille as the only acceptable position to put it.

The suspension was virtually standard MGA, though stiffened, the Lockheed drum brakes had special linings, and the optional centre-lock wire wheels were specified.

Clearly MG would have a hard job even to qualify at Le Mans in 1955, as their minimum target speed was just under 80 mph and they would have to cover at least 1,915 miles in the 24 hours. They could not even be expected to win their class as they were

The purposeful nose of the new MG shown at Le Mans in 1955. In all major structural areas it was identical with the proposed production MGA, but at the front the recesses let into the metal pressing to accommodate the big bumpers were smoothly panelled over, while a powerful Lucas Flamethrower lamp was added to one side of the radiator grille to help pierce the notorious early-morning mists.

faced by a battery of very special racing Porsches. Their low weight would help (they were claimed to weigh only 1,600 lb dry — very much less than their actual weight in race trim) as would their good shape, but more power would obviously have been a bonus.

Nevertheless, it would be interesting, for technical purposes, to see how they would perform against the team of works-prepared Triumph TR2s, which might be heavier and somewhat less special, but had the benefit of 2-litre engines.

For MG, the 1955 Le Mans race was both a triumph and a disaster; for the world, the event was a complete disaster. In more recent years, MG managers have pointed out that it would have needed an outright victory even to make an impression over the holocaust which overtook the race when Levegh's Mercedes-Benz 300SLR plunged into the grandstands opposite the pits, bursting into flames, killing more than 80 people, and injuring hundreds more.

If one can ignore the carnage in this event, and for the purposes of this survey I must, it becomes clear that the MGA 'prototypes'

performed splendidly. Of the three cars which started, two finished, and the third (driven by Dick Jacobs and J.J. Flynn) suffered a mysterious crash at White House when Dick Jacobs was driving, only minutes after the Mercedes crash had occurred. No apparent reason for this has ever emerged, but it is thought that Jacobs might have been distracted by the turmoil facing him as he rounded the corner before the pits straight.

The other two cars, driven by Ken Miles/Johnny Lockett, and Ted Lund/Hans Waeffler, finished strongly and reliably, in 12th and 17th positions, fifth and sixth in their class. The leading MG averaged 86.17 mph and covered 2,082.78 miles. It was an astonishingly successful debut, and the cars gave virtually no trouble. Perhaps the biggest mistake committed all week was that the cars were presented for race scrutineering with the wrong competition numbers painted on!

The Triumph TR2s, incidentally, were convincingly defeated, even though they had much larger engines and were running with very effective disc brake installations. The best of the TR2s finished 14th, 56 miles behind the leading MGA.

The Le Mans disaster, of course, cast a pall over the entire motor sporting scene, and in the next few months there were wholesale cancellations of events. One of the biggest casualties was the French Alpine Rally, for which one or more of the Le Mans cars might have been entered. This explains, incidentally, why the 'prototype' Le Mans cars had both doors when only one was really needed, and why they had provision for all the usual all-weather equipment like a full-size screen, hood and sticks and side-screens. The passenger door was permanently closed at Le Mans, but not welded to the main shell as was once stated. The Le Mans cars were so easily reconverted to standard that LBL 303 (No 64 at Le Mans) was loaned to *The Autocar* for their use in July. The Le Mans engine was retained for this job, but the production car's gearing (a 4.3 axle and the wide-ratio gearbox) was fitted.

In September, as part of their agreed competition programme, three EX182s — two Le Mans cars (LBL 301 and LBL 303) and the race-prepared spare machine (which replaced the badly-damaged Dick Jacobs car) — were entered for the Tourist Trophy race on the Dundrod road circuit in Northern Ireland. The cars were unchanged structurally and in body layout, but most excitingly two of them were fitted with experimental twin-cam

Pictured in line-astern in the 1955 Le Mans race are the Lund-Waeffler (64) and Lockett-Miles (41) MGAs. The latter car finished in 12th place, having averaged nearly 87 mph for the 24 hours, often in very slippery conditions. This was a near-faultless performance which incidentally beat the best of the 2-litre Triumph TR2s by 56 miles. Although the 1955 Le Mans cars officially were prototypes, their light-alloy bodies were of exactly the same shape as the future production MGA. The bonnet straps and the streamlined rear-view mirror housing are very neat detail fittings.

engines, neither having been seen in public previously.

These engines, respectively, were prototypes of the Palmer/Morris Engines design already detailed in the previous chapter, and of the Appleby/Austin Company design. Both were actively being developed (effectively there was a design competition in progress in BMC between the Austin and Morris factions) and considered for use in future BMC production cars, the MGA among them. The Twin-Cam unit from Morris was in much the same visual form as it would take when on the market in 1958. There are more details about the entirely special Austin-inspired engine in Chapter 7.

In preparation for the Tourist Trophy race, both engines were installed in tuned form, fitted with racing exhaust systems, special cooling arrangements, and with twin dual-choke Weber carburettors (which would eventually cause problems). Though both were designed to the same brief, they were visually quite different; the Morris Engines design had angular camshaft covers, while the Austin's covers had more rounded contours. Valves on the Morris unit were opposed at 80 degrees, and on the Austin at 66 degrees.

Taking advantage of the prototype regulations under which the cars were still being entered (the MGA's public launch would follow the week after the TT had been run), one car (LBL 301) was raced with modified frontal styling, including lowered and much smaller headlamps. This, however, was a change not to be seen again.

Both engines were in trouble even before the race itself. The unproved Austin engine was found to have a rev-limit no higher than that of the race-tuned pushrod B-series unit and it produced very little more power. Even before the cars were shipped to Northern Ireland, therefore, it was removed and replaced by a Le Mans-type B-Series engine.

LBL301, the first of the lightweight Le Mans cars, was given a modified nose in time for the Tourist Trophy race in September 1955 in an attempt to provide it with better aerodynamics. Mounted in that position the lowered headlamps would certainly have been illegal for British road use, and would have been almost ineffective for giving a good spread of light, but the Tourist Trophy was a daylight event in which such things were not critical. Note that the Flamethrower light had been discarded and that this car was running with front-wheel disc brakes; this was also the car in which the prototype Twin-Cam engine was installed. Full road equipment (screen/hood/sidescreens) was added after the race.

The Palmer-Morris Motors engine, therefore, was the only prototype twin-cam engine to race at Dundrod, in the low-headlamp car depicted above. However, it was in constant problems due to the fact that special inlet manifolds fabricated to suit the Weber carburettors had hairline cracks. This eventually ruined the air-fuel ratio to the engine and the car had to be retired.

The only MG finisher, of the two pushrod-engined cars to race, was the Jack Fairman/Peter Wilson car, which finished 20th overall and fourth in its class. Even though, as at Le Mans, the best of the MGs had beaten the best of the Triumph TR2s this

was little consolation.

Like Le Mans, too, the Tourist Trophy was marred by a big accident. A multiple crash which involved seven cars resulted in the death of two drivers, and in a later crash another driver was killed. This sort of thing could only give sports-car racing a bad public image, and BMC's top management decreed that there should be no more official MG entries in top events. This did not stop one or two clandestine entries being slipped through, nor (in later years) did it stop cars being prepared for the North American BMC subsidiary to use at Sebring, but the overall effect on the MGA's competition programme was that it had to concentrate on rallying.

In October 1955, however, Abingdon had one more chance to show off the paces of their new cars. In a mass visit to the Montlhéry banked circuit, near Paris, six different BMC models were unleashed to show that they could all complete more than 100 miles in one hour of high-speed motoring. There were three saloons (Austin A90, Riley Pathfinder and Wolseley 6/90), an Austin-Healey 100 and two MGAs, one a production car and the other a road-equipped Le Mans car.

Racing driver Ken Wharton drove the production car, which completed 102.54 miles in one hour from the standing start, while the 'racing copper' John Gott completed 112.36 mph in the Le Mans car after one false start when a tyre burst at three-quarters distance. The weather was frightful, with driving rain bucketing down throughout the runs, which made the achievements all the more creditable.

The Le Mans cars were not used again by the factory, who built up no fewer than five new machines for the 1956 season. Their first event was the Mille Miglia (a race, for sure, but enough of a long-distance 'rally' to convince the BMC management that an entry was acceptable) — an event which MG had not contested since the great days of 1933 when the supercharged MG K3 Magnettes had made their triumphal debut.

Peter Scott-Russell/Tom Haig drove MJB 167 to second place in its class, while Nancy Mitchell/Pat Faichney took third place behind them; the class winner was an exclusive and expensive Porsche Speedster. All this, incidentally, was in the 'limited price' class. As Marcus Chambers subsequently commented: 'We ought to have used the Le Mans cars and gone for an outright class win.' Mechanically the two cars were almost standard apart from the fitment of a vast fuel tank, high axle ratio, oil cooler and the stripping off of bumpers. Each carried the distinctive 'Cyclops' lamp on one side of the radiator grille.

With hopes high for a good rallying career, all five of the new cars — one white, the rest bright Italian red — started the Alpine Rally. Although it was an event where numerous cars won *Coupes des Alpes* for unpenalized runs, MG fortunes were mixed. John Gott's car was shunted at an early stage, and later broke a half-shaft (probably as a result of the same shunt), while near the end of the event Jack Sears up-ended his car on a mountain descent. Three cars finished, and it was Nancy Mitchell, using her rebuilt Mille Miglia car, who won a *Coupe des Alpes* and also took the *Coupe des Dames*.

In September, three of the four cars entered finished the gruelling Liège-Rome-Liège rally, which went nowhere near Rome, but *did* visit the rugged depths of Yugoslavia. The cars were beaten for pace, as they had been on the Alpine, and it was John Gott's car (MJB 191) which finished 13th, with John Milne's car 14th.

Even by 1957, when the motoring scene was somewhat soured by the aftermath of the first Suez war and the petrol rationing which followed it, Abingdon found themselves in the horns of a dilemma. While the MGA 1500s were strong and handled beautifully, they were not nearly fast enough, especially when faced with competition from the 1,600cc Porsches in the same class. At Abingdon, too, the lusty six-cylinder Austin-Healey 100/6 was finding favour, and showed signs of being a potential outright winner if developed with determination.

1957, therefore, was a thin year for MG rally cars. Nancy Mitchell was third in the *Coupe des Dames* in the Tulip Rally, while on the Liège-Rome-Liège John Gott took 14th place (MJB 167 — the old 1956 Mille Miglia car), and Nancy Mitcehll 16th place (in OBL 311). There was no Alpine Rally in 1957, nor even an RAC Rally.

That was the bad news. The great news was that by dint of these and other performances, Nancy Mitchell became European Ladies Champion in 1957, as she had been in 1956. Nancy mainly used MGAs, but also dabbled in Magnettes where the class and handicap situations encouraged it. Her wins followed those of Sheila Van Damm and preceded those of Pat Moss — truly this was the decade when British girls were supreme in the

An interesting detail shot of the other twin-overhead-camshaft engine tried in a lightweight MGA at the 1955 Tourist Trophy race. This unit was completely Austin-designed by W.F. Appleby's team at Longbridge and had no common parts with any existing Austin or Morris engine. Carburation was by twin dual-choke Webers and the cooling system (not complete when this picture was taken inside the racing department at Abingdon) included a large header tank mounted on the scuttle. This engine was never again seen in public.

rallying business.

With the Austin-Healeys getting better and better it was decided to cut back on works MGA competition, and all the push-rod-engined cars were sold off. Only once in 1958, when John Gott finished ninth in the Liège in the first of the works Twin-Cams, was there an official entry. The Twin-Cam specification

Alongside the Austin twin-cam engine at the 1955 Tourist Trophy, MG also tried the true Twin-Cam prototype engine for the very first time. For this event it used twin-choke Weber carburettors and already it carried the MG octagon on its inlet camshaft cover. Compared with the engine which went into production in 1958 it is different in many details, but not in general layout. As with the Austin engine, note the separate scuttle-mounted cooling header tank, and note the water outlets from the centre of the head, which were eliminated on production cars. Gerald Palmer conceived this conversion at Cowley.

looked promising for a rally car, and without the overall excellence of the Austin-Healeys to distract them the Abingdon preparation kings might have made more of it.

That first car (PRX 707), however, was only used once more, on the 1959 Tulip Rally when John Gott's navigator made a navigational error which dropped him well out of the results at the finish. There was a 1959 sister car (RMO 101), which John Gott drove in the 1959 Monte Carlo Rally and crashed, which John Sprinzel/Stuart Turner misnavigated on the Tulip, and which John Sprinzel crashed on the Acropolis of that year — it was not a lucky car.

With one very honourable exception, therefore, that was the end of the MGA's European competitions career. The exception was that wonderful MGA 1600 Mk II De Luxe Coupe (getting the title absolutely right is worth it in this case!) which was built to Stuart Turner's orders for the 1962 season. Turner was Marcus Chambers' successor to the chair of BMC competitions manager from September 1961 and, while a great enthusiast for the big Healeys, he was not blinded to other BMC cars.

The 1600 Mk II, with its 1,622cc engine, was now in the 1,601-to-2,000cc class, and if used in De Luxe specification could have four-wheel disc brakes and centre-lock disc wheels. Further, Turner had taken advantage of the latest international rules which allowed optional carburettors to be specified. For this car, therefore, he homologated the single sidedraught twin-choke Weber carburettor, which helped to boost the power to about 115 bhp if the free-flow exhaust manifold and the high-lift camshaft profiles were also specified.

This particular Coupe, 151 ABL, contested only three events, with three different crews. In January the Morley twins won their class in the Monte Carlo Rally. Better still, they finished second in the entire Grand Touring category, and even that was no disappointment to BMC as the winner was a works Austin-Healey 3000 driven by David Seigle-Morris.

In the Tulip Rally, in May, the car was crewed by Rauno Aaltonen/Gunnar Palm, was driven absolutely on the limit up the dozens of timed hill-climbs, and won its class narrowly from the entire team of new 2-litre TR4s entered by the reopened Triumph Competitions Department. It has to be said in the Triumphs' defence that their engines were then absolutely standard, but even so Aaltonen was giving away 369cc, and he

After their introductory 1955 season at Le Mans and in the Tourist Trophy, Abingdon's Competitions Department concentrated on using the MGA in rallies. One of the stalwarts of the team was Nancy Mitchell, who won the European Ladies' Championships in MGAs and ZA Magnettes in 1956 and 1957. Here she is, with co-driver Pat Faichney scrambling back on board, restarting from a control on the Alpine Rally in the Italian Alps. The team cars that year were mainly painted bright Italian red — the theory (proved to be effective) being that Italian policemen and level-crossing keepers would assume they were Italian cars and give them priority of passage! In later years this colour descended into Abingdon tradition, so that the famous Austin-Healey 3000s, MGBs and Minis were all painted the same colour. Mrs Mitchell won the *Coupe des Dames* on the 1956 Alpine, and her car was equipped with the removable hardtop and sliding sidescreens, even though they had not then been made available to the general public. This was product-proving in the most arduous manner, and it also allowed the MGA to run this event as a Grand Touring car.

made light of the job.

ABL's final outing was in the 1962 Liège, when John Gott drove the car, but unfortunately it did not finish. The Liège, by then, was a real breaker's yard test of a strong car, and the dice were heavily loaded against *any* car finishing.

MG's competition effort then gave precedence to the MGB, which had just been announced, and the fortunes of these very versatile machines is described in Chapter 6.

Apart from building their own rally cars, Abingdon also found time to build racing-specification MGAs during the winter for the BMC North American company to use at the Sebring 12 Hours race in March. It was almost traditional that new cars should be prepared, that they should race at Sebring, and that they should then be sold in North America. For that reason I have not included the cars in my list of individual machines at the end of this chapter.

A team of MGAs started the Sebring race in 1956, and similar cars were entered the next two years, but as far as is known now these had no connection with Abingdon. In 1959, however, four Twin-Cam Coupes were sent across to Florida, where the best pair took second and third places in their class. A year later two Twin-Cam Tourers (fitted with detachable hardtops and carrying, for a short time, the numbers UMO 94 and UMO 95) made the journey, but were not rewarded with any success.

Even after the Twin-Cam had been discontinued, Sebring was not forgotten. For the 1961 event a pair of 1600 Coupe De Luxe models (complete with knock-on disc wheels and four-wheel disc brakes) were sent to America, where they took first and second places in their class, the class winner being driven by J. Parkinson/J. Flaherty. Finally, in 1962, three more 1600 Coupe De Luxe models made the trip, and the two best performances were second and third places in their class.

Team captain in 1956 and until the end of 1961 was the well-respected and well-liked 'motoring policeman', John Gott. He drove MJB 191 with Chris Tooley into 13th place in the rugged and gruelling Liège-Rome-Liège of 1956, the car being virtually standard apart from the use of the hardtop and sliding sidescreens. There was much discussion on the merits of pressed-steel or wire wheels; pressed wheels stood up to more punishment from bad roads, but took longer to change after a puncture. As the factory usually carried plenty of spares, the team cars were usually fitted with quick-release wire wheels, and bent rims or broken spokes were treated as disposable items.

The intriguing detail about these cars is that although the 1600 Mk II had already been announced, the cars sent were built to 1600 Mk I specification. There was no good marketing reason for this, but the sporting reason was that by building 'new' obsolete cars, the Mk Is could be entered in the under-1,600cc class and therefore stand a better chance of success.

The only other works car, though Abingdon always made strenuous efforts to say that it was privately owned, was the Twin-Cam — SRX 210 — which Ted Lund raced at Le Mans on three successive occasions — 1959, 1960 and 1961. Lund, we recall, had been a member of the successful 1955 team who raced the aluminium-bodied MGA prototypes.

The story really begins in 1956, when MG had been hoping to enter one or other of the two advanced projects which they had under wraps. One was a car with a production chassis converted to De Dion rear suspension, but with an entirely special body (that was EX186), while the other used a spare light-alloy MGA-shape body, but with a tubular-frame chassis (that was EX183). Both cars were to have used the prototype Twin-Cam engines, as the Austin-designed twin-overhead-camshaft engine had now been abandoned.

BMC's abandonment of racing meant that both cars had to be shelved. EX186 (the special-shaped car) was sold to North America, while EX183 was dismantled. Ted Lund, who had been asked to make himself available to drive the specially-shaped car (which hung around until 1958-59), then decided that he would like to drive at Le Mans again, but in a standard-looking Twin-Cam.

Abingdon, therefore, agreed to build a new race car, a Twin-Cam Tourer, and it had a light-alloy bodyshell. The origins of this particular shell are not now clear, but it is thought to be the remains of one of the original 1955 shells, still left lying around at Abingdon. Although the car was in every functional way works-built and prepared, BMC company politics meant that it had to be entered privately by the North-West Centre of the MG Car Club.

In its first year, looking standard apart from the carburettor air intake to the right of the grille and its lowered perspex screen, it ran fast until Colin Escott (co-driving) had the misfortune to hit a large alsatian dog at high speed on the Mulsanne straight, which killed the unfortunate animal and destroyed the car's cooling

One of the most intriguing non-works factory cars, if I may mix things up a little, was the MGA Twin-Cam used by Ted Lund to race at Le Mans in 1959, 1960, and 1961. Although the chassis was MGA Twin-Cam, the original bodyshell was a standard-shape open version, but was in fact one of the ex-1955 light-alloy Le Mans car shells. The car, in theory at least, was always a private entry, though significantly enough it was registered by MG and carries one of their familiar 'RX' numberplates. For 1960 the body was altered substantially. Don Hayter, now Abingdon's chief engineer, utilized MGA Coupe doors and wind-up windows, and modified an MGA Coupe roof so that a fast-back body was evolved. Whereas the car originally had a special shallow MGA Tourer screen in 1959, with the fast-back style it used a standard MGA Coupe screen with a fair degree of wrap-around. In 1959 the car retired after it had collided with an unfortunate dog (this smashed the radiator and the engine cooked itself). In 1960 — coloured, incidentally, in the same light green as used on the famous mid-engined EX181 record car and with a race-tuned Twin-Cam engine enlarged to 1,762cc — the car won the 2-litre class and averaged 91 mph for the 24 hours. In 1961, with the final body modifications to the nose shown here, its engine blew up, but not before it had lapped Le Mans at 101.66 mph.

A three-quarter-rear view of SRX 210, taken in the 1970s when the car was running on non-standard wide-rim wheels, shows off the sleek lines of the fast-back shape. From the nose back to the rear line of the doors the shape is standard MGA Coupe, but the tail is changed substantially. In this guise the car was capable of 140 mph, and the Twin-Cam engine could produce nearly 130 bhp.

In spite of BMC's general disapproval of entering MGs in racing, Abingdon usually managed to build cars for the Sebring 12-hours sports car race, where they were entered by BMC's North American subsidiary. Although these two Coupes, prepared by the factory at the beginning of the year for the 1961 race, look like Twin-Cams, they are actually pushrod-engined 1600s, using the Twin-Cam chassis, brakes and wheels. These cars, therefore, are two of the rare De Luxe models, which were built in both 1600 and 1600 Mk II guise. Marcus Chambers made sure that all the right items were homologated for competition use. In the 1961 event the two cars took first and second place in their appropriate Sebring GT class.

For the 1962 Sebring race BMC built three new 1600 Coupes, their drivers being (left to right) Jack Sears, Bob Olthoff and Sir John Whitmore; Andrew Hedges and the two American drivers Flaherty and Parkinson were not present for this picture. On this occasion, however, the cars had no success. The actual cars are an intriguing mixture. The current production model at the beginning of 1962 was the 1600 Mk II, with the recessed grille bars, but these three cars were built with the old-style grille, but with alternate bars removed to aid radiator cooling. As in 1961, they were De Luxe models, running with Twin-Cam-type chassis, four-wheel disc brakes and centre-lock road wheels. They were also among the very last MGA Coupes ever built. The bumpers have been removed to aid streamlining and to minimize vehicle weight (the regulations allowed this).

52

A shattered-looking John Gott and a very chirpy-looking Ray Brooks with the first of the works Twin-Cam rally cars at the end of the very gruelling 1958 Liège-Rome-Liège rally, in which they had just taken ninth place. Apart from its 20-gallon fuel tank, special seats and a host of detail fittings to make maintenance and operation easier, this Twin-Cam was absolutely standard, and the high-compression engine showed no temperament when running on the awful Jugoslavian petrol of the period. The Twin-Cam could undoubtedly have been a fine and successful rally car, but at Abingdon it was rapidly overshadowed by the massive 3-litre Austin-Healeys and was never fully developed.

Rauno Aaltonen's phenomenally nimble MGA 1600 Mk II De Luxe kicks away the chock as it starts a Tulip Rally speed hill-climb in May 1962. This was the final success for a works MGA, where the young Finn (with Gunnar Palm as his co-driver) won his class and defeated a complete team of 2-litre Triumph TR4s. The same car had already competed in the 1962 Monte Carlo Rally (when the Morley twins had won their class) and it would be used by John Gott on the Liège-Sofia-Liège without success. At the time the regulations allowed bumpers to be removed, and this had made the car look even more sleek than normal. This was one of the few MGA Coupes used by Abingdon — they normally preferred detachable glass-fibre hardtops.

Syd Enever used a spare prototype EX 175 MGA-type chassis-frame and suspensions to form the basis of the new MG record-breaker, EX 179, built in 1954. The frame was extensively drilled to lighten it as much as possible. This overhead shot of EX179 shows the unsupercharged MGTF 1500 engine, the very forward-placed water radiator and the header tank on the left side of the scuttle area. The road wheels were standard TF items, but the back axle, with straight-cut gears, was entirely special. Later in its life this car was fitted with a prototype Twin-Cam unit (1956), a prototype Sprite engine (1957), and finally was re-born as EX219, an 'Austin-Healey', in 1959.

system and fried the gearbox.

For 1960 the Le Mans rules changed, and since they demanded deeper windscreens it was thought that a full coupe top would be an advantage. The car was therefore given a wraparound Coupe screen, Coupe doors and drop glasses, and a fast-back hardtop styled by Don Hayter using the existing contours of the Coupe top as its base. All this was done at very reasonable cost, even though Lund had now officially bought the car from the factory. The engine was bored to 79.4 mm, which resulted in a capacity of 1,762cc, was given Weber carburettors, and with a 4.1 axle ratio proved capable of pulling 130 mph. Thus equipped the car finished the 1960 race 13th, won its class, averaged 91 mph and set a best lap speed of 99.46 mph.

A year later the car was back at Le Mans, this time with a modified nose, headlamps pushed back a few inches along the wings and even more power (128 bhp). Now it was capable of 140 mph in a straight line and really looked splendid, but unfortunately the heavily-modified engine let go in a big way after the car had recorded its first 100 mph lap at the circuit — 101.66 mph to be precise. Although it was intended to enter the car at Le Mans in 1962, this did not prove possible, and therefore it was retired to the less glamorous fields of club racing.

SRX 210 lives on, one of the few ex-works MGAs to retain its very definite personality, and is thoroughly representative of the way Abingdon could turn a good road car into a formidable racing machine.

Works competition MGAs — 1955 to 1962

1955	LBL 301	LBL 302	LBL 303) Four original race
	LBL 304		) cars with light-alloy
			) bodies

1956	MRX 42	MRX 43	MJB 167	MJB 191
	MBL 867			
1957	MJB 167	OBL 311		

— all the above were MGA 1500s, where appropriate with detachable hardtops

1958   PRX 707 — a Twin-Cam with detachable hardtop

1959   PRX 707   RMO 101 — a Twin-Cam Coupe

1960   777 ENK — an MGA 1600 on loan from John Gott

1962   151 ABL — an MGA 1600 Mk II De Luxe

In addition the factory sometimes built new cars for use in the Sebring 12 Hours race, where they were campaigned by BMC's North American subsidiary. In later years these cars were as follows:

1959 : 4 Twin-Cam Coupes
1960 : 2 Twin-Cam Tourers (with detachable hardtops) —
        UMO 94 and UMO 95
1961 : 2 MGA 1600 Coupe De Luxe (with Twin-Cam chassis, etc)
1962 : 3 MGA 1600 Coupe De Luxe (with Twin-Cam chassis, etc)

Note: Between 1959 and 1961, Ted Lund drove a Twin-Cam at the Le Mans 24 Hours race. Though truly a sponsored private entry, it was registered at Abingdon — SRX 210. In 1959 it ran as a Tourer, while in 1960 and 1961 it ran as a modified Coupe with a fastback style.

The victorious team of privately-prepared MGA 1500s after winning the Team Prize in the 1956 Sebring 12-hours race — the MGA's first big event in production-car form. The drivers were Ash/Ehrman (No 49), Spittler/Kincheloe (No 50) and Allen/Van Driel (No 51).

An American MGA in company with a works-prepared British Lotus Eleven during the 1957 Sebring race. This is one of the MGAs which performed so well in the major international event the previous year.

CHAPTER 4

MGB — the modern classic

1962 to date

Even by 1958, and before the MGA 1600 had been put into production, Abingdon had had thoughts about a new model to replace the MGA. After one serious attempt to provide the existing MGA chassis with a completely new body (this was EX214, which is described in Chapter 7), work began on a car with a completely new structure. By 1959 the MGB project — coded EX205 by Abingdon, ADO23 by BMC — was under way.

Apart from its body shape, the MGB was also to be distinguished by its unit-construction body/chassis structure. It wasn't the first-ever monocoque British sports car (even by 1959 the little Austin-Healey Sprite and the Sunbeam Alpine were so equipped), but it was the first ever tackled by Abingdon. Experience with other BMC monocoque models (the Abingdon-assembled Magnettes, for instance) suggested that considerable weight savings might be gained; the MGA's chassis, though admirably strong, was also very heavy. Combining chassis and bodyshell made technical *and* financial sense, even though the cost of tooling would be very high. Recently John Thornley has confirmed that this capital cost was going to be *too* high, and that he got approval for the car by agreeing a more politically reasonable cost, then paid Pressed Steel a higher price for every body delivered. Because the MGB has carried on, very successfully, for much longer than even MG managers had hoped, Pressed Steel's accountants must now be delighted.

In 1959, EX205 was first schemed out with all-independent suspension (soon discarded, even at the drawing stage), then with coil spring/radius arm location to its MGA-type live axle, but in the end a conventional leaf-spring location was chosen.

At one time it was hoped that the new car could be ready by the end of 1961, and later it was firmly forecast for production at the very beginning of 1962, but eventually the public launch came in September 1962. The first 12 production cars were started in May 1962, and a further 138 followed in June 1962. All but two of the first 500 cars were earmarked for North America, the other two being test and publicity cars for the MG company itself.

The shape of the MGB was finalized by a lengthy, but logical, process of development, starting from the basis of the ultra-smooth EX181 record car of 1957. Don Hayter, who was then an MG body engineering specialist, but later was to be put in charge of all design engineering, recalls that the first car was shaped (as a quarter-scale wind-tunnel model) with reference to EX181, but with necessary road-car items like a radiator grille, headlamps and passenger space blended in as carefully as possible.

This car, however, was shaped around the existing 7ft 10in MGA wheelbase, and was thought to be altogether too large and too bulbous. It was Hayter's task to pare this shape down, by reducing the wheelbase to 7ft 7in, and to make it smaller and lighter. In its original guise it had a backward-sloping radiator grille, MGA-style, but the more aggressive (and now familiar) MGB style evolved for two reasons — one was because the designers liked it that way, and the other was that it allowed a bigger radiator to be fitted. It also gave more potential space for larger and longer engines to be fitted at a later date; the question of six-cylinder units was already being discussed, though it would be years before a definitive MGC project evolved.

In the beginning, design went ahead with two engines in mind — the 1,622cc ohv B-Series unit already slated for the MGA 1600

The now-familiar lines of the MGB, which caused such a sensation when the car appeared in 1962. This was one of the very earliest production cars, appropriately enough in left-hand-drive form as it was intended for the export market, and it shows to perfection how that original bulbous prototype proposal had been pared down to an acceptable and quite timeless shape for quantity production.

The original MGB Tourer production car of 1962, showing that the only detail badging — apart from the proud display of the MG octagon — was placed on the boot lid. The filler cap on the MGB was placed low down relative to the old MGA layout, and the boot compartment was more spacious. The car was shorter in the wheelbase and altogether more squat than the MGA. Uncharacteristically, the rear bumper fits very badly on this car.

Mk II, and the existing 1,588cc Twin-Cam unit. Before long, however, the Twin-Cam engine was dropped altogether, and work was concentrated on the pushrod design. The MGB, as everyone knows, has always been built with the 1,798cc engine, and although Abingdon knew of this unit's existence when they started work on the MGB, they originally preferred to keep it in reserve for a later MGB development.

However, although the MGB's structure was efficiently laid out, it soon became clear that it would result in a car slightly heavier than the last of the MGAs, and that without another engine boost this would mean a drop in performance. It was therefore decided to rush through the bigger engine for the MGB, even though it would not be used by any other BMC car until 1964, and then not in the same guise or structural condition.

At 1,798cc, this B-Series engine derivative was the final stretch ever offered to the public (although MG themselves would race very special over-bored 2,004cc engines later in the life of the MGB). Compared with the 1,622cc engine — 76.2 x 88.9mm bore and stroke — the latest version had a bore and stroke of 80.26 x 88.9mm; the stroke, as on every other B-Series engine ever sold, never changed from this dimension, which in prosaic British Imperial measure is 3.5 inches.

This engine stretch was achieved by siamezing all the bore castings in the cylinder-block except for a slim water passage between the second and third cylinder barrels. Ten years earlier this would have worried the production engineers enormously; modern casting techniques allowed the new castings to be controlled well, and distortion has never been a serious problem with the unit. To look after the increased power output (up from the 86 bhp and 97 lb ft of torque on the last MGA to 95 bhp and 110 lb ft torque on the MGB) the main bearing diameters were increased from 2.0 to 2.125 inches.

The MG cylinder-head, valves, valve gear and manifolding were all unchanged, though the carburettors were re-needled and new Cooper paper-element air cleaners were specified. To achieve an 8.8:1 compression ratio the new pistons had concave crowns; one of the most obvious tuning modifications was to call for flat-topped pistons which helped to raise the ratio.

Engine oil temperatures were higher in the MGB than they had been in the MGA, so an oil cooler, mounted ahead of the water radiator, was standardized for export models and made optional

Not a line or a detail out of place in the original MGB, which is a shape of which Abingdon is rightly proud. It is as attractive today as it was in 1962. Note the mirror support rod, which looks almost as if it is a divider for the wide curved windscreen.

on the home market (it was standardized on all cars from the autumn of 1964, coincident with the introduction of the five-bearing engine).

Although the MGA had been a great and lasting success, everyone at Abingdon was determined to surpass this achievement with the MGB. This meant that even more attention had to be paid to production engineering and cost control than ever before. The unit-construction bodyshell, to be made only in two-seater tourer guise at first, was an obvious result of this policy, and it also helps to explain why the only light-alloy skin panel in the MGB was the bonnet pressing.

More interior space than in an MGA, but not really room for useful occasional seats behind the front seats. No hood is fitted to this example as it is all set to receive the optional hardtop, which had fixings slotting into the fastening immediately behind the door shut face. A non-standard prototype two-spoke steering wheel is fitted to this car.

Apart from the non-standard steering wheel this is the facia layout familiar to MGB enthusiasts all over the world. The radio, of course, was (and remained) an optional extra. It was nice to see that the map-reading lamp was carried over from MGA to MGB, but the passenger could no longer operate the horn, which now lived in the centre of the steering wheel.

The structure was a miracle of compact packaging. Compared with the MGA the wheelbase had been cut by three inches, as had the overall length. On the other hand the pedals and the passenger toe-board had been moved forward by six inches; the floor was even lower than it had been on the wide-chassis MGA, and as the scuttle and seats had all been relocated relative to the back wheels there was a good deal of space for luggage (or willing tiny children!) behind those seats. The seats themselves were wider than before, and the cockpit width had been increased by a couple of inches in spite of the bulkier doors with their new-fangled wind-down glass windows. Facia styling was quite new, and one most obvious change was the position of the horn, which was now in the steering wheel boss instead of in the centre of the facia, as had become traditional on the MGA range.

Apart from the increase in engine size, the MGB was mechanically very similar to the MGA. The gearbox was internally the same as before, with no synchromesh on first gear. Because the driver was seated further forward there was no need for a special MG gearbox extension, and the lever fitted neatly into the standard BMC casting layout. The back axle, similarly, was structurally as before, though the MGB was treated to a higher (3.909:1) ratio than any offered with the MGA.

The suspension looked very familiar, though there were many differences in detail. Because of the monocoque structure, the MGB was given a sturdy detachable front cross-member, which supported the entire front suspension and steering units. This cross-member, incidentally, had been welded to the rest of the structure on the very first prototype car. Apart from development changes to the king-pin, and softer settings for springs and dampers, the layout was recognizably descended from that of the YA, TD, TF and MGA models.

There was a lot of spare air space ahead of the water radiator, which was mounted on a steel diaphragm linking the inner wheel-arches, though nobody thought anything of this at the time. The boot, because its lid was much more horizontal and because the rear wings did not drop away as much, was a lot more capacious than that of the MGA. All was not luxury, however, as the lid had to be propped open by a short stick, and there was no cover over the flat spare wheel, which made luggage stowage awkward, particularly if the optional wire wheels were specified.

There was a comprehensive facia layout, as we had all come to

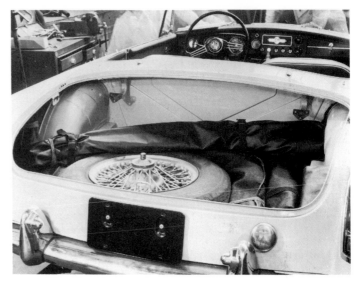

An early-production MGB, fitted with the optional wire-spoke wheels and showing the shape of the boot. This was one of the original cars with a build-it-yourself hood stowed in the boot compartment. Later a fold-down hood was standardized.

expect from a sporting MG, with neat provision for the optional radio. The fresh-air heater (it drew its air from a decorated slot at the base of the windscreen) was an option, costing £16.85. In Britain, the basic price of the MGB when it was released in the autumn of 1962 was £690 (total, with tax, £950), which compared very favourably with £750 for the Triumph TR4, £695 for the Sunbeam Alpine and £865 for the Austin-Healey 3000 Mk II.

Among the extras (often fitted in build, as the Abingdon records confirm) were the heater and wire wheels already mentioned (the wheels cost an extra £34.37) the oil cooler, a front anti-roll bar and a folding (in place of a build-it-yourself) hood. The Competitions Department, of course, could carry forward all their accumulated knowledge of the B-Series engines and transmissions from MGA usage, and tuning items were made available almost at once.

Because the cars had been in production since June 1962,

deliveries got under way at once following public release in September; the pipeline to the United States and Canada was already full by then. More than 4,500 MGBs left Abingdon before the end of 1972 — a figure, incidentally, which exceeded the number of MGAs built (3,049) between January and July. In 1963, the MGB's first full year, and without any supply problems of any serious nature, no fewer than 23,308 cars would be produced. This was not quite an Abingdon record (the number of MGAs built in 1959 — 23,319 — beat this by a mere 11 cars, although 1,519 of these were Twin-Cams), but it surpassed the entire prewar production achieved by MG between 1923 and 1939! Demand, and Abingdon's capabilities, were certainly continuing to expand.

Compared with the last of the MGAs — the 1600 Mk II — there was a measurable, if not a sensational, performance boost. The MGB's maximum speed was better by two or three miles an hour, the standing-start quarter-mile time was trimmed by a few tenths of a second, and the top-gear performance was slightly better in spite of higher overall gearing. Of equal importance was the fact that fuel economy had suffered very little, if at all, and even a small penalty depended on the way in which the new car was driven.

It was undeniable, however, that the MGB was an altogether 'softer' car to drive. With as much, if not more, available wheel movement, coupled with softer springs and damper settings, the MGB was so much easier on its occupants than the MGA had been. Yet the handling and the response were still right up to traditional Abingdon standards. Without wishing to push my metaphors too far, one could say that this was certainly a triumph for MG.

The British opposition — particularly Triumph and Sunbeam (who had been selling hard on their own new-found refinement and appointments for the past year or so) — were horrified. They had been having enough trouble in selling their modern cars against the ageing MGAs, but now, faced with the MGB, they were in real trouble. As far as they were concerned, the only consolation was that no hardtop was immediately available, nor was there a coupe model.

Number-noters will want to know that the MGB chassis sequence starts at G/HN3 101, while the original 1,798cc engines were Type 18G at first, becoming 18GA when fitted with closed-

This is the engine bay of a late-model MGA 1600 Mk II, shown for comparison purposes with . . .

... the MGB engine bay. The MGB bonnet opening is much wider, and access to the engine for service and maintenance is much improved. The later 1,798cc engine is visually very similar to that of the Mk II's, 1,622cc unit, except for new routing of pipes, cables and other details, and for the new Coopers air-cleaners with their spouts, one facing forward and one back. No heater was fitted to the Mk II depicted, whereas the MGB shown has its heater and associated piping in place. The two big pipes at the far side of the engine bay lead to the front-mounted engine oil-cooler. This, of course, is a left-hand-drive car, as evidenced by the brake and clutch reservoirs to the bottom right of the picture.

circuit crankcase breathing at the beginning of 1964.

Production of the body/chassis units, as with so many such things in the BMC organization, was a rather complicated business. All the pressings were stamped out at the Pressed Steel factory at Swindon (Pressed Steel, who also welded-up the floorpan, was still an independent concern, and would not fall into the BMC net until 1965, just before the announcement of the MGB GT), but sub-assemblies were then transported to the Morris Bodies Branch factory in Coventry for assembly. Once painted there, they were then returned to Abingdon, in multi-loads by transporter lorries, for final assembly to their mechanical components.

In the meantime, engines and transmissions were being machined in different BMC factories in the Birmingham area, while suspension components and radiators came from other locations. The MGB, in this respect, was even more of an 'assembled' car than the MGA, for virtually nothing of any importance was actually manufactured at Abingdon.

This, of course, is quite excusable and readily explained. The MGB was being built, right from the start, at a rate of nearly 500 cars a week. At the same time, something like 250 Sprites, Midgets and Austin-Healey 3000s were also pouring off parallel production lines at Abingdon. The little factory, as purchased by William Morris at the end of the 1920s, was simply not intended to cope with this scale of production — 50 cars a week was thought to be a good rate in the 1930s, and 200 cars a week was normal before the MGA was launched in 1955 — so the only way that build rates could be pushed up was by contracting out almost all manufacturing operations.

The problem, even so, looked like becoming even more acute,

and without the construction of extensive new premises there appeared to be no easy solution. As we know, no new production buildings were to be built at Abingdon in later years. More and more capacity, however, was to be squeezed out of existing buildings — one important move being to have the completed bodyshells painted *and* trimmed before they reach Abingdon. Withdrawal of the Austin-Healey 3000 would help, but it would not be until 1970 that 50,000 cars of all types were built in a single calendar year.

There were two big jumps in the expansion process. The first came with the launch of the MGB (22,751 cars of all types were built in 1962 and 35,495 followed in 1963). The second came at the end of the 1960s, following rationalization and the demise of the big Healey (38,007 cars in 1968, 47,736 cars in 1969 and 51,676 in 1970). Abingdon's all-time record stands at 55,639 cars (1972), of which 39,393 were MGBs. From then on production eased a little, to the order of 42,000 to 46,000 in any 12-month period over the next few years.

After it was launched in 1962, therefore, the MGB's success story scarcely faltered, and it continued to dominate the Abingdon scene. However, it would be wrong to suppose that the same car was being built in say, 1978 as was launched in 1962. If that were so, the MGB would not have continued to sell so well, and there would certainly have been no point in preparing this book. The life story of the MGB is not of a car which was launched and which lived happily ever after. It is a car which has been changed progressively over the years.

Apart from its basic layout, and a percentage of the parts, almost everything in the car has been improved, changed, or generally modified since then. The MGB, in fact, is already something of an institution, a philosophical combination of VW Beetle and Morgan. You may be sure, too, that even as this is being written, new recruits are joining the ever-increasing army of MGB devotees.

The basic motor car remained in production for 18 years, during which period there had been one basic body innovation (the MGB GT), one major restyle (the introduction of those vast black bumpers for the 1975 model-year), a new gearbox (1967), an automatic gearbox option (1967 to 1973) and a new rear axle (1965 for the GT and 1967 for all other cars). There had been no actual engine transplant, but almost everything else — wheels,

rims and tyres, facia styling, seats, cooling arrangements, steering wheel and dozens of other details — have come in for attention.

All this has to be noted, so that dedicated MGB lovers can sort out their particular loves (and hates?), but it makes no sense merely to fight our way through it in chronological order. Instead, I have prepared a series of tables — one listing development changes introduced as and when they were ready, and the others summarizing the 'model-year' improvements — and I have also decided to summarize the main changes in each mechanical section of the car; and if the rest of this chapter begins to read rather like a technical description, I'm sorry.

The model line-up

The MGB was announced in September 1962 and was available then only as an open Tourer. A glass-fibre detachable hardtop became available within a matter of months (and of course proprietary tops also began to flood the market) but there were no other body variations until 1965. Apart from the introduction of optional Laycock overdrive at the beginning of 1963 there were no important mechanical options, either.

From the autumn of 1965, the Tourer was joined by the MGB GT coupe, which was and remains a sleek and very practical three-door hatchback. This, although mechanically similar to the Tourer, had certain basic differences which would not be incorporated in the Tourers for some time. These are explained below.

In the autumn of 1967 the MGB was joined by the six-cylinder MGC (described in more detail in Chapter 5), and at the same time it was uprated in various mechanical ways to become the Mk II, the principal improvements being an all-synchromesh manual gearbox and the offer of automatic transmission as an option.

From the start of the 1970 model-year there were noticeable styling changes, and equipment alterations which included the specification of reclining seats. This model, still called the Mk II, was easily picked out by its recessed and restyled radiator grille and its sculptured Rostyle road wheels.

The next big change was for the 1972 model-year, when the car became known as Mk III. Almost all the visual changes were to the interior, with facia improvements and more storage space provided. An energy-absorbing steering column became optional on British-market cars.

Assembly of MGB Tourer bodyshells at the Morris Bodies Branch, Coventry, in 1966. All the pressings were produced by Pressed Steel at Swindon, but welding-up, painting and, for a time, trimming were carried out in Coventry. Batches of bodyshells were then delivered to Abingdon by transporter for final assembly. The use of a light-alloy bonnet panel is clear, but all other panels are in steel.

For 1973 the grille was restyled again, and there were other cosmetic improvements. The MGC had been dropped in 1969, but in the summer of 1973 (effectively at the start of the 1974 model-year) the MGB was joined by the MGB GT V8, which is also detailed in the next chapter. At the same time the American version was fitted with energy absorbing over-riders, radial-ply tyres were standardized for world markets, a brake servo was fitted to British-market cars and the unsuccessful automatic transmission option was deleted.

Changes for the 1975 model-year were introduced in two phases, such that there is a short series of car known as 1974½ by the MG staff. The 1975 cars had the controversial and very noticeable black polyurethane mouldings to act as front and rear bumpers, and the cars were rejigged to stand noticeably higher off the ground (this was to meet bumper-height regulations in the US market). At the same time the 'federal' engines began to be fitted with a single Zenith-Stromberg carburettor (power had now been strangled down to only 65 bhp, which was no more than that developed by an MGA 1500 in 1955), and there was a new type of

overdrive. At this point, too, the MGB GT was withdrawn from the American market.

For 1977 there was a completely restyled facia with a new instrument layout and control positioning, the suspension settings were revised, there was a four-spoke steering wheel, and many other decorative and functional improvements.

The single most important equipment change not introduced with the start-up of a model-year programme was the standardization of overdrive (previously it had been optional) in June 1975, just before the end of the 1975 model-year build programme. This was inevitable, as by then 99 per cent of all MGB orders has specified the optional overdrive.

Apart from the last 1,000 LE models, built in 1980, the final series of MGBs were all very much the same as those built since the start-up of 1977 model-year production.

Bodyshell and structure
From 1962 to 1971, MGB bodyshells were assembled at the Morris Bodies Branch factory in Coventry from complete

Surely no praise from me is needed to describe the really classic lines of one of the world's most popular closed sports cars? Compared with the Tourer, the MGB GT had a much larger windscreen, and was even more comfortable and well-appointed inside. Wheel rims were wider than those fitted to the Tourer, and the car was rather heavier due to the generous equipment and the steel top.

The MGB GT was styled initially at Abingdon, but sent to Pininfarina for his detail attention and for construction of the first prototype. The production car seen here was as elegant a fast-back sporting car as had yet been seen in Britain, and was still selling strongly 23 years later. Announced in 1965, it was not the first of the hatchback sports cars (the Aston Martin DB2-4 took that honour) but it was certainly one of the most practical. The basic chassis engineering was as for the MGB Tourer, except that the GT was the first of the growing range to be given the more robust Salisbury axle, while a front anti-roll bar was standard. The angle of the rear window is absolutely critical in relation to its cleanliness in dirty weather, and a great deal of attention was paid to this at the wind-tunnel stage.

Rear detail of the first series of MGB GT, showing the very useful tailgate, top-hinged and self-supporting when opened. The *very* occasional seat could be unlatched and folded forward, thus increasing the size of the loading/luggage area.

floorpans and panel sets supplied from the Pressed Steel factory in Swindon. Pressed Steel also completely assembled the first batch of MGB GTs. Since 1971, because of the closure of the Coventry bodybuilding facility, bodies have been stamped *and* assembled at Swindon, taken to Cowley for painting and trimming, and then sent on to Abingdon for final assembly.

Apart from the many smaller changes, the two big junctions have been when the MGB GT variant was phased-in in the autumn of 1965, and when the 'black bumper' cars were introduced for the 1975 model year.

The MGB GT is much more than a Tourer with a coupe roof. The screen is deeper than that of a Tourer, and the engineering of the floor pan is significantly changed to allow the fitment of an occasional (*very* occasional, to tell the truth) rear seat, which can be folded to give extra loading space. Because of the different roof outline, too, the door glasses and other such details are unique to the GT. From the autumn of 1965 until the summer of 1967 the GT also had under-floor differences to accommodate the bigger Salisbury-type rear axle, which was only commonized with the Tourer in the summer of 1967.

Many enthusiasts have discovered, to their dismay, that the introduction of black bumpers brought many sheet-metal changes behind those bumpers, which make it impossible (or at least economically inadvisable) to revert to chrome bumpers.

From the beginning of the 1975 model-year American regulations meant that the bumpers had to be placed at a certain height. The only way to do this without making the whole car look ridiculous was to lift the entire shell relative to the ground. This increased the ground clearance by 1.5 inches (and raised the car by the same amount), and this was achieved by revising the fixing and pick-up points for the rear springs and the front cross-members. This means that there are important differences between pre-1975 and 'black bumper' cars in the suspension/bodyshell area.

Cars for America have also had their unique reinforcing items for some years (notably, for instance, the longitudinal pressed-steel beams inside the door skins to allow the car to meet side-intrusion legislation), and these cars, of course, are much more numerous than those built for other markets. In the ten years to the end of 1977 more than 300,000 MGBs were produced, of which more than 200,000 were originally delivered to North

The spare wheel of an MGB GT lives under the loading floor as shown in this picture of the original prototype. The baulk of timber holding up the load floor is *not* standard!

Reverse lights were standardized on all MGBs from April 1967, fitting very neatly into the tail panel near the rear-lamp clusters.

America.

Numerically, too, cars with the Salisbury axle and the modified bodyshell are considerably more common than those fitted with the B-Series MGA-type axle (of which about 100,000 were built, none of them MGB GTs).

Engines

From 1962, when it was introduced, to 1980, when it was finally discontinued, the MGB was powered by one or other version of the BMC/BL B-Series engine. This unit stems from an engine introduced by Austin in 1947, and has been used in many other BMC or Leyland cars. Even though it was rendered obsolescent by the new overhead-camshaft O-Series engine of 1978, that engine was not fitted to MGBs. I drove prototype cars in that year with twin-carb O-Series units installed, but the decision to kill-off the MGB strangled that development.

The 1,798cc engine has a bore and stroke of 80.26 x 88.9mm (nominal), with a cast-iron cylinder-block and a cast-iron cylinder-head having siamesed inlet ports and a siamesed centre exhaust port. Until Chassis No. 48765 the engine had a three-bearing crankshaft, but all subsequent engines have had five bearings.

Development changes have usually been concerned with the requirements of the North American market, and this has meant that over the years there have been no attempts to make the unit more powerful. Rather, successful work to reduce exhaust emissions have resulted in a substantial reduction in power for the North American engines, and slight reductions (scarcely noticeable in road use) for European versions. The MGB, of course, has been exported only to North America since the beginning of 1977.

Original engines were Type 18G, but closed-circuit crankcase breathing was introduced from Chassis No. 31021 and the units became Type 18 GA. When BMC introduced the front-wheel-drive Austin 1800 in the autumn of 1964 it had a five-bearing engine, and this cylinder-block was standardized on MGBs from Chassis No. 48766; these engines were Type 18GB.

From the introduction of the G/HN4 cars (the Mark II models introduced in October 1967) the engines became Type 18GD, or 18GF where exhaust-emission controls were fitted. From the introduction of the G/HN5 cars (October 1969) the designations became 18GG, or 18GH with exhaust-emission controls. The

Take your eyes off the girl and concentrate on the features of this 1972 model-year MGB Tourer! At this juncture the facia was mildy restyled, with face-level air vents being added to the centre, which meant that provision for the optional radio had to be made in a revised gearbox tunnel centre-panel which still provided space for the radio speaker. Reclining seats had been standardized in October 1969, while the facia layout had already been re-arranged at that point and a smart leather-rimmed steering wheel with satin-finish perforated light-alloy spokes had been added. Other improvements included the centre console surrounding the gear-lever (automatic transmission, incidentally, was still available), and the provision of an oddments box with a lift-up lid between the seats. New on this model, too, were the rocker switches (in place of tumbler switches) made necessary by the latest legislation and changing fashion. The headrests were not standard on most versions of the car.

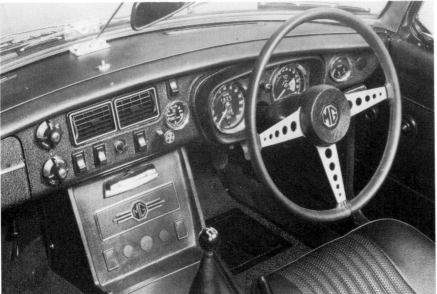

From October 1969 the MGB was mildly restyled externally, with British Leyland badges on the front wings, the addition of pressed-steel Rostyle wheels (wire wheels were still optional) and a recessed style of front grille. The car shown is a 1972 model-year example (subsequently called the first of the 'Mark III' cars, though this nomenclature does not have wide acceptance) on which no further changes had been made.

1972 models were given this facia and instrument panel in non-federal territories. Obvious changes include the location for the optional radio, the panel which now supports it, the provision of swivelling face-level cold-air vents where the radio used to live, and the revised rocking-type switches. A smart interior lamp had replaced the central map light in the autumn of 1970.

From the start of the 1973 model year, in October 1972, there was a new style of steering wheel — the forthcoming V8 would have a similar wheel but without the spoke slots — black-painted wiper arms and blades, a cigarette lighter as standard and padded armrests on the doors. The general layout of the interior and controls was not changed. Note the brushed-nylon seat facings, standardized from the late autumn of 1971, while the slim oddments box had been added in 1972 and has been a feature ever since.

The 1973 model-year MGB GT interior, showing the seats and the continuing presence of tiny but useful occasional rear seats. This seat's back-rest, of course, could be folded down to give more space for stowing luggage or perhaps even dogs.

For the 1973 model-year cars, MGB abandoned the recessed grille which had been in use from the autumn of 1969 and reintroduced a more conventional MG-like grille. It was, however, quite distinctive, for although the familiar octagon was back in prominence on a chrome bezel, the main grille was a discreet black mesh. Rostyle wheels were retained as standard and rubber-faced over-riders were a feature. This picture confirms that the detachable hardtop was still offered, and had changed hardly at all since 1962.

final change was in 1971 when 18GK and 18V was applied to different specifications of engine for different markets.

Until the introduction of 1975 model-year cars all MGBs had twin SU carburettors (of several different detail types, depending on the market for which the car was built), but since then all American-market machines have been fitted with a single Zenith-Stromberg Type 175CD carburettor.

Since the start of the 1971 model-year, MGBs for America have had exhaust-port air-injection (the air pump is belt-driven and is mounted on the front of the engine), and a closed evaporative-loss fuel system. Since the introduction of the Zenith-Stromberg carburettor the engines have also had exhaust-gas recirculation systems, and for California deliveries only a catalytic converter in the exhaust system.

In this section, too, I should mention the fuel supply position. When the car was announced it had a 10 (Imperial)-gallon fuel tank, but this was increased to 12 gallons from Chassis No. 56743, in March 1965. From the start of the 1977 model-year (from Chassis No. 410001), cars have been delivered with an 11-gallon tank.

Transmissions

The MGB was introduced with the same gearbox as had always been used in MGAs, with the deletion of the special gear-change extension casting, which was no longer required because of the more forward seating position arranged for the MGB. The internal gear wheels, synchromesh cones and other details were all exactly as had been used in the last MGAs.

The Mk II MGB was introduced in October 1967 (Tourer : Chassis No. 138801, GT:139824) and with it came a brand new all-synchromesh gearbox. In general layout, in casing dimensions and in many internal components (including the gear wheels and the synchromesh details) it was commonized with the six-cylinder MGC and the Austin 3-litre saloon (ADO 61), both of which were announced at the same time. The important difference was that the six-cylinder cars had a different casing to mate with the redesigned 2,912cc engine, while the MGB version was unique in that it had to mate with the cylinder-block of the B-Series engine.

This gearbox was used on all subsequent MGBs (and on Leyland light commercial vehicles which use the B-Series engine), but as several sets of gear ratios have been used, these are

The most dramatic and controversial change in styling to date was the introduction of the big flexible soft-bumper layout on 1975 model-year cars. At the same time the whole structure was lifted further to give standardized bumper heights (USA regulations being the culprit, as they so often have been in recent years). The changes to accommodate the bumpers are more far-reaching than might at first appear. Although the main pressings — bonnet, front and rear wings, and boot lid — were not changed, there were hidden revisions and all manner of new fixings. It is not easy (but it can be done if you are determined) to return a rubber-bumpered MGB to the earlier chrome-bumper condition. Tail-lamp revisions were introduced at the same time.

detailed below:

MGB ratios 1967-1974: 1.00, 1.382, 2.167, 3.44, rev 3.095 (also non-o/d MGC, 1967-68 and early Austin 3-litre)

MGB ratios 1975-1976: 1.00, 1.382, 2.167, 3.036, rev 3.095

MGB ratios 1977-on: 1.00, 1.382, 2.167, 3.333, rev 3.095

and, for comparison purposes:

MGC ratios, o/d 1967-1968, all cars 1968-1969 (also later Austin 3-litre): 1.00, 1.307, 2.058, 2.98, rev 2.679

MGB GT V8 ratios: 1.00, 1.259, 1.974, 3.138, rev 2.819

Overdrive was available as an option on all MGBs built from the beginning of 1963, whether with the original B-Series or the later all-synchromesh gearbox. The overdrive was standardized (with a price adjustment) from June 1975. After the important facia redesign introduced for 1977 model-year cars, the overdrive switch was included in the gear-lever knob (Triumph-style). On all cars built before then the switch had been mounted on the extreme right of the facia (right-hand drive) or on the extreme left

(left-hand drive).

For many years the Laycock overdrive used carried a step-up ratio of 0.802:1 (which gave an overall ratio of 3.13:1), but from Chassis No. 367901, from the beginning of the 1975 model-year, the later Laycock LH overdrive was fitted, with a step-up ratio of 0.82:1 and an effective overall ratio of 3.20:1.

From the introduction of the Mk II MGB (effectively phased-in at the same time as the all-synchromesh manual gearbox) there was the additional option of Borg-Warner Type 35 automatic transmission. This was only possible due to the revised and reshaped floorpan of the Mk II/MGC models — there is no way that automatic transmission can be fitted into an *unmodified* Mk I bodyshell.

The Borg-Warner's internal ratios were 1.00, 1.45, 2.39, reverse 2.09 — and these were usually matched with a 3.7:1 rear-axle ratio, compared with 3.909 for all manual-transmission cars.

The automatic transmission was not a sales success and was

In the summer of 1975, to celebrate British Leyland's own interpretation of the 50th Anniversary of the start of MG production, a special series of MGB GTs — 750 in all — were built as 'Anniversary' specials. Mechanically they were standard, but every car was painted in British Racing Green with special gold striping. All were four-cylinder models, but they were given MGB GT V8 road wheels, 175-section tyres, head restraints, overdrive and tinted glass.

Apart from the special colouring and the gold detailing, another recognition point of the 1975 Anniversary special MGB GTs was the MG octagon badge fixed to the front wings above and ahead of the corporate British Leyland badge.

withdrawn at the end of the 1973 model-year. Of more than 180,000 MGBs built in the 1967-1974 period, only about two per cent (perhaps less than 4,000 cars) were built with automatic transmission.

Two distinct designs of rear axle have been used in MGBs. The original axle, the B-Series corporate component, was virtually identical with that fitted to all MGAs built from 1955 to 1962 except for minor details like brake fixings and pipe runs. It was used on all MGB Tourers up to Chassis Nos. 129286 (wire wheels) and 132462 (disc wheels).

With the introduction of the MGB GT, however, a new Salisbury-type axle, bigger, more robust and with an entirely different construction, was introduced. This was common with the MGC component in layout (though the ring/pinion gear was different) and would also be adapted for use in the MGB GT V8 cars of 1973-1976. All MGB GTs have this axle, and the Tourers inherited it immediately after the Chassis Nos. already quoted. Significant bodyshell changes were needed to accommodate this big axle, so that it is difficult (if not eventually impossible) to adapt an earlier MGB Tourer shell to the later axle.

More than with most long-running models, however, it is important to know chassis numbers when looking for spares and replacements. The MGB Mk II, for instance, is significantly different in the region of the gearbox tunnel and toe-board from the Mk I (this was to accommodate the new manual and automatic gearboxes); the cars built after the start of the 1974 model-year were also changed in the engine bay area to commonize as much as possible with the V8-engined cars; and a quick glance at the illustrations in this book will show how much the detail layout of the engine bay (with respect to radiator type, radiator position, overflow tank, brake servo, and dozens of other details) has changed over the years.

There simply is not space in this book to go into that sort of detail, but I have, at least, been able to summarize the main, 'building block' modifications over the years. If, too, there had only been one basic motor car to be considered, my task would have been more simple. Two variants of the MGB, however, the six-cylinder MGCs and the V8-engined MGB GT V8s, have been produced in quantity alongside the four-cylinder cars, and these are considered in some detail in the next chapter.

By 1975 model-year the USA-specification MGBs had been forced to adopt a single Zenith-Stromberg carburettor to keep abreast of the tightening anti-pollution laws, as is clear from this production-line shot taken in the autumn of 1975. By 1977 the engine-driven fan had also been discarded, and current USA-spec MGBs have two electrically-driven and thermostatically-controlled fans ahead of the water radiator. In this picture the radiator and the oil-cooler have yet to be installed.

1965 model-year improvements
Five-bearing engine replaced three-bearing engine.
Oil cooler standardized.
Electronic rev-counter fitted in place of mechanically-driven item.

1968 model-year improvements
Introduction of Mk II model, with following changes:
All-synchromesh gearbox.
Optional Borg-Warner Type 35 automatic transmission.
Alternator fitted in place of dynamo.

The first of the 1976 model-year GTs (by then confined to sale on the British market) showing the relatively high stance off the ground, and — just visible — the 'GT' flash standardized on the rear quarter behind the side windows.

Energy-absorbing steering column (USA market).
Special facia style (USA market).
Dual braking system (USA market).
Negative-earth electrics.

1970 model-year improvements
Styling changes include recessed-type radiator grille.
Corporate British Leyland badges on front wings.
Rostyle wheels in place of original steel wheels (wire-wheel option continued).
Minor re-arrangement of facia controls.
Reclining seats.

1971 model-year improvements
Uprated heater and revised air ducting.
Addition of interior courtesy light.
Automatic boot and bonnet opening stays.
New hood mechanism (Michelotti-designed).
Emission equipment including engine-driven air pump (USA-market).

1972 model-year improvements
Introduction of Mk III models with following improvements:
Revised facia layout with repositioned auxiliaries and tumbler switches.
Face-level fresh-air vents.
Centre console surrounding gear lever.
Oddments box between seats.
Brush-nylon seat facings.
Collapsible energy-absorbing steering column optional (non-USA market).

1973 model-year improvements
New radiator grille with chrome surround and black mesh.
Rubber-faced over-riders.
Leather-trimmed alloy-spoked steering wheel.
Black-painted wipers.
Cigarette lighter.
Tonneau cover standard on Tourer model.
Door arm-rests.
Radial-ply tyres standardized (British market).
Heated backlight standardized (British market).

1974 model-year improvements

New energy-absorbing rubber over-riders (USA market).
Hazard warning flashers (British market).
Brake servo standardized for British market.
Automatic transmission option withdrawn.
Radial-ply tyres standardized (all markets).

1974½-1975 model-year improvements

(These changes were introduced in two phases — in September 1974 and December 1974):
Soft-bumper (polyurethane mouldings) style incorporated.
Single Zenith-Stromberg carburettor for federal (USA) market.
Raised ride-height suspension.
One 12-volt in place of two 6-volt batteries.
Catalytic converter added to exhaust system (USA California).
Collapsible steering column now standardized (all markets).
Twin-stalk steering-column controls standardized (all MGBs).
V8-type instrument pack standardized on four-cylinder MGB.
MGB GT deleted from North American market.
LH overdrive specified instead of original D-Type.

1977 model-year improvements

Completely restyled facia layout including grouped instruments.
Electric clock added to specification.
Pedal-pad positions changed to allow 'heel-and-toe' operation.
Striped fabric seat trim standardized.
Halogen headlamps (British market).
Tinted glass on MGB GT.
New heater control layout and ancillary changes.
Small-diameter four-spoke steering wheel.
Suspension changes including front and rear anti-roll bars.
Thermostatically controlled electric cooling fan (two for federal cars).
Separate radiator catch tank.
Overdrive switch on gear-lever knob.
Seat head restraints standardized.

Important MGB development changes

From time to time significant improvements have been made to the basic MGB design. Although it has not been possible to list minor changes, the main milestones, with chassis-number details,

For 1977 there were further important revisions to MGB facia/control layout. In the centre-console area, an electric clock was new, the console itself was reshaped, there was a revised interior light, new heater control positions and other details. The overdrive had been standardized since June 1975, and in this restyle the location of its switch was moved to the centre of the gear-lever knob, as had been common on many British Leyland models (notably Triumphs) in recent years.

The 1977 model-year MGBs introduced striped-fabric seat trims, a feature which was carried over to the headrests which were now standard. The gear-lever console and the oddments box were carried on, and the new car was given a smart new four-spoke steering wheel. Not visible here is a revised main facia, in which all dials are grouped ahead of the steering wheel in a very neat fashion.

The engine bay of a 1977 model-year home-market MGB, showing that although the basic layout was still virtually the same as it had always been, there were many significant development changes. New for 1977 was the thermostatically-controlled cooling fan (just visible ahead of the radiator), a revised radiator, a cooling catch tank (on the right side of the engine bay just behind the radiator support diaphragm) and other details. Even the radiator position had been moved relative to its position in 1962.

A special instrument layout and facia layout was chosen for MGBs destined for North America. Introduced along with the Mk II cars, this was used until the mid-1970s. It featured a padded crash roll ahead of the passenger seat, different instrument faces and dial groupings, but there was no glove box or stowage space, which many thought a disadvantage.

are listed below:

Change and Date	From Chassis Number
July 1962: MGB model announced	101
August 1963: Folding hood standardized	19586
February 1964: Closed-circuit crankcase breathing	31021
September 1964: Five-bearing engine introduced, along with oil cooler and electric rev-counter	48766
March 1965: 12-gallon fuel tank replaced 10-gallon tank	56743
October 1965: MGB GT model introduced	71933
November 1966: Front anti-roll bar standardized on Tourer model	108039
July 1967: Salisbury-type rear axle (always fitted to GT) standardized on Tourer models	
— with wire wheels	129287
— with disc wheels	132463
Summer 1967: Reversing lamps standardized on all cars after Tourer body 100414, GT body 016928	—
October 1967: Mk II MGB range introduced with all-synchromesh gearbox and many other changes	
— Tourer	138801
— GT	139824
October 1969: Styling and equipment revisions for 1970 model-year.	187211
August 1970: Styling and equipment revisions for 1971 model-year	219000
January 1971: Seat belts fitted at factory instead of by dealers	233393
May 1971: Mk III version of MGB announced with styling and equipment changes for 1972 model-year	258001
May 1972: Single-handed-operation seat belts fitted	282420
August 1972: Styling and equipment revisions for 1973 model-year	294251
September 1973: Equipment revisions for 1974 model-year including deletion of automatic transmission option. Radial-ply tyres standardized, all markets	328101
September 1974: Styling and equipment revisions for 1974½ model-year including raised suspension and moulded polyurethane bumpers	360301
December 1974: Equipment revisions (mainly for USA federal cars in regard to engines) for true 1975 model-year. LH-type overdrive standardized	367901
June 1975: Overdrive fitment standardized	
— Tourer	380278
— GT	379495
September 1975: Start-up of 1976 model-year cars	386601
June 1976: Styling and equipment revisions including completely restyled facia for 1977 model-year cars	410001
September 1977: Equipment revisions for start-up of 1978 model-year	447001
October 1980: Last MGBs built	
— Tourer	523001
— GT	523002

CHAPTER 5

MGBs with more muscle

MGC and MGB GT V8

Since the MGB was announced there have been two periods when more powerful versions, with larger engines, have been on sale, and there have been other tentative experimental attempts to provide similar cars. The first — the MGC — was a qualified failure because it had lost the 'Abingdon touch', while the second — the MGB GT V8 — failed because it could not be sold at a price low enough to attract the typical Capri customer.

Even before the MGB was announced, in 1962, it was clear that its chassis and stiff monocoque structure could handle quite a lot more performance, so long as the excellent overall balance was lost. However, I must stress that the MGB was designed strictly 'all of a piece'. Its layout, its structure, its suspensions and its engine bay, were all designed to make the 1,798cc car as good as possible. The idea of putting bigger, heavier and more powerful engines into the car came later.

The six-cylinder Austin-Healeys (the 100/6 at first, the 3000 later) had been assembled at Abingdon since 1957, and although they were progressively improved and made faster their styling was virtually unchanged. By the mid-1960s BMC policy vacillated (and I can think of no less wounding word than this) between approving a new Austin-Healey model, a modified Austin-Healey with different engines, an Austin-designed sports car with Hydrolastic suspension and a Rolls-Royce engine, or a new joint model, with Austin-Healey and MG badges as appropriate, based on the MGB.

Eventually, and not without considerably confusion, it was decided to phase-out the 'big Healey', the Austin-Healey 3000, at the end of 1967, by which time it was effectively to have been replaced by derivatives of the MGB with similar-sized six-cylinder engines. I must make it clear, however, that the new car was not related to the Austin-Healey in any technical way except in the original design roots of the 3-litre engine.

Events which affected the choice of new engines are mentioned in Chapter 7, but at this stage I must summarize the car's conception and birth. In the beginning — that is to say in 1963 and 1964 — BMC knew no more than that they desired to see a bigger-engined MGB introduced; further, they wanted this to be marketed in MG and Austin-Healey forms. At this very early stage, therefore, Donald and Geoffrey Healey were drawn into the scheme of things, as it happens much against their better judgment. In the initial concept period, therefore, there were two projects — ADO 51 was the Austin-Healey version, and ADO 52 the MG version, the visual difference always being confined to grille and nose shapes.

One engine proposed was the old Austin-Healey 100 2.6-litre four-cylinder unit (a scheme swiftly discarded), and this was followed by a plan to use BMC-Australia's 2,433cc six-cylinder unit, which had three SU carburettors and was effectively one-and-a-half B-Series 1,622cc units. This engine, as any BMC engine expert will confirm, is a completely different 'six' from the C-series 3-litre.

It is easy enough to say that it was then decided that a modified C-Series six-cylinder should be slotted into the basic MGB bodyshell (there were too many economic, spares/service and political problems against the use of the Australian 'six'), but the engineering was not at all as straightforward as that. Indeed, when this engine had been first proposed, it was clear that it would involve a major front-suspension redesign, and that even

The six-cylinder MGC was launched in 1967, and was produced in Tourer and GT form for the next two years. Nearly 9,000 cars were built — more than 100 each week — but the car was not thought to be successful enough for the company to persevere with it. There were many engineering differences under the skin, some still not completely understood even today by MG fans, but the styling was almost entirely unchanged. From the front, as can be seen, only the bonnet bulges and the larger — 15-inch — road wheels, looked at all new.

The bonnet panel of the basic MGB design was given a bulky hump to provide clearance for the MGC's six-cylinder engine, and in addition to this it was necessary to provide local clearance (the streamlined bulge surmounting the main hump) to clear the front SU carburettor. Apart from this there were no badges on the nose of the MGC to identify it from its smaller-engined cousin.

One major MGC chassis innovation was the use of torsion-bar independent front suspension. In this view the new bottom wishbones and the longitudinal torsion bars running back to anchorages under the seats can be seen clearly, along with the front anti-roll bar, which was a standard fitting. The bulk of the six is obvious for that is an engine pulley *ahead* of the line of the anti-roll bar.

when certain changes were made to the engine the MGB's smooth bonnet line would still have to be reprofiled to allow clearance over the front of the bulky engine.

Without changes to that engine (for it could not be pushed back any further along the chassis, nor could it be pushed down) there probably would never have been an MGC model at all. However, BMC decided to conduct a major redesign of the engine in connection with a new saloon car (ADO 61 — a new Austin 3-litre), which enabled Syd Enever's engineers to tackle the problem with a bit more confidence.

The old BMC C-Series six-cylinder engine, therefore, would be phased-out in 1967, at the same time as the Austin-Healey 3000 was withdrawn, and a 'new' six-cylinder engine would be phased-in for the Austin saloon and the new MG/Austin-Healey sports car. Announcement was fixed for the autumn of 1967 in each case.

In fact the car took a long time to get into production. There had been thoughts about big-engined MGBs even before the MGB was announced in 1962, and the first mention of ADO 52 in Abingdon's 'Modification Note' system occurs as early as July 1964. Mention of Austin-Healey equivalents, and the GT versions, followed over the next couple of years.

The Healey family were never altogether happy with the idea of a 'badge-engineered' MGC carrying their old car's illustrious name (it was to have been called 'Austin-Healey 3000 Mk IV'), but it was not until the autumn of 1966, after both models had been released for production, that the ADO 51 Austin-Healey version was dropped. Geoff Healey still retains the general-arrangement drawings of this car in his files.

The first ADO 52, or MGC, prototype was built during 1965, and the first true production cars followed in July 1967. In fact the first 13 pre-production cars (not the higher figure sometimes

The 2,912cc six-cylinder engine used in the MGC was by no means the same as that found in the Austin-Healey 3000s, as this overhead shot of the engine installed in the car makes obvious. To get the engine into the basic structure the MGB radiator-support panel had to be scrapped and a new radiator position was evolved in the extreme nose of the car, with a new cross panel, and with the engine oil-cooler ahead of that. On the scuttle, the brake servo and the brake/clutch pedal boxes swopped sides if a left-hand drive car was built. Fixings for the telescopic shock absorbers (unique to the MGC) can be seen on the inner wheel-arch.

quoted elsewhere) were built at the end of 1966 for further development and testing. Chassis numbers began at 101 for open cars and 110 for GTs.

Although the MGC, superficially, looks like the MGB (and indeed it shares almost all the skin panels, decoration, trim, and many inner and structural members) there are important engineering differences. These were made, not merely to be different or more modern, but to make installation of the 2,912cc six-cylinder engine feasible.

The engine, incidentally, was built by the BMC Engines Branch factory at Coventry; design (or, more strictly, redesign) had been carried out there to Alec Issigonis' brief. By comparison with the old C-Series engine, it had seven main bearings instead of four, had rejuggled cylinder-centre positions, and consequently was about 1¾ inches shorter than before; it was also claimed to be 44 lb lighter than before, though this gain was much less than had originally been promised from Morris Engines, and was still 209 lb heavier than the MGB engine it replaced.

Superficially it looks similar to the old engine as used in the Austin-Healey 3000, and of course the dimensions (83.34 x 88.9m, 2,912cc) are the same. There were, however, important cylinder-head changes to allow extra 'federal' detoxing equipment to be added without difficulty, and the extra internal friction generated by the seven main bearings meant that the maximum power and torque (145bhp at 5,250rpm and 170 lb ft torque at 3,400rpm) were very slightly down on those of the Austin-Healey (150bhp at 5,250rpm and 173 lb ft torque at 3,000rpm). Nevertheless, these were still 53 per cent and 55 per cent, respectively, better than those of the MGB's 1,798cc engine.

Behind the engine was the new all-synchromesh gearbox — brand new, with a new case, new internals and new selection arrangements — shared with the Mk II MGB introduced at the same time, and also incidentally shared with the Austin 3-litre, which was announced in October 1967 but only staggered into production in the summer of 1968.

Although the MGC's life was to be short, its transmission variations were complex and need sorting out. As these affect both internal gear ratios *and* back axle ratios, I should point out that the original arrangements lasted up to about the half-way point, and that revised arrangements were phased in from Chassis

The MGC's 2,912cc engine, as introduced in 1967 and ready to be fitted to a car in production, showing off the alternator position, the pre-engaged starter on this particular unit, and the vertical mounting of the oil filter. The unions for the oil-cooler pipes have been blanked off with tape while the engine was spray-painted. The brand-new all-synchromesh gearbox (shared with the Austin 3-litre but by no means common with the all-synchromesh MGB unit) is fitted but this assembly has no overdrive. The slim air-cleaner housing has yet to be fixed to the twin SU carburettors.

Nos. 4236 (GT) and 4266 (Tourer).

First, when the car was introduced, there were two sets of *internal* gearbox ratios. Manual cars used ratios of 1.00, 1.382, 2.167, 3.44, and (reverse) 3.095:1, while overdrive cars used 0.82 (with overdrive engaged), 1.00, 1.307, 2.058, 2.98, and (reverse) 2.679:1. The first of these sets, incidentally, was common with the set used in the all-synchromesh MGB; the manual set was shared with the early-model Austin 3-litre cars, while the overdrive set was shared with later model Austin 3-litres.

After the mid-model changes, however, all MGCs were fitted with the close-ratio set of gears. The original laudable object had been to provide idealized ratios with or without the overdrive; later it became apparent that the engine had enough torque to shrug off such minor nuances of engineering.

There was the option of a Laycock overdrive (with a step-up ratio of 0.82) which worked on top and third gears, and the further option (also introduced on Mk II MGBs) of the Borg-Warner Type 35 automatic transmission.

The back axle, shared in general layout, if not in detail, with that of the latest MGBs (in other words it was the Salisbury-type)

had various ratios, also changed at the same chassis number junction. To avoid confusion, these are annotated as follows:

Original cars	Without overdrive	3.07
	With overdrive	3.31
	With automatic transmission	3.31
Later cars	Without overdrive	3.31
(from Chassis Numbers	With overdrive	3.7
4236 (GT) and 4266	With automatic trans-	
(Tourer))	mission	3.31

It is worth noting, too, that for competition use, Abingdon's Competitions Department asked for, and were provided with, the following special ratios: 3.58, 3.9, 4.22, 4.55, 4.875. They were also provided with an ultra-close set of internal gearbox ratios which could have been (but never were) applied to works MGBs.

The biggest and most important changes, however, were to the structure and the suspension of the basic bodyshell. This was done purely on account of the bulk and excessive weight of the big six-cylinder engine. Changes, too, were commonized with the

Mk II MGB (those, for instance, necessary to make space for the all-synchromesh gearbox or the automatic transmission).

Because the engine/gearbox joint face could not be moved back along the drive-line (if it was, this would mean the gearbox being moved back, too, which would have reduced space for the passengers), the extra length of the six-cylinder unit had to be accommodated in the nose of the bodyshell. This meant that the steel diaphragm placed across the MGB's engine bay, which supports the cooling radiator, had to be eliminated, and a new cross-panel packed up against the nose supported the new radiator and the oil cooler.

Bodyshell changes — some commonized with Mk II MGBs — were much more wide-ranging than might at first have been thought. The sheer bulk of the six-cylinder engine meant that the MGB's sturdy detachable cross-member could not be used, and the shallower and less rigid member which could be fitted was not

strong enough to cope with the increased vehicle weight and the normal suspension loads.

While retaining a basic wishbone suspension geometry, therefore, suspension loads were taken by longitudinal torsion bars connected to the lower wishbones (there are some similarities to the familiar Jaguar XK and E-Type systems), these being fixed by adjustable mountings to a pressed cross-member under the front seats. There is no question of torsion bars being used because they were better than coil springs for the job in hand — their installation was merely easier and more convenient. Another innovation in the front suspension was the use of telescopic instead of lever-arm hydraulic dampers — the only instance so far of such dampers being used on a derivative of the MGB family of cars. An anti-roll bar was standard, and rack-and-pinion steering was retained, but with less direct gearing (3.5 instead of 2.9 turns lock-to-lock of the steering wheel) both because of an installation

Detail of the MGC gearbox extension, in this case with the optional overdrive in place. The mechanical speedometer drive is operated by a skew-gear at the rear of the overdrive's output shaft.

Automatic transmission was made available as an option when the MGC was announced, and it was introduced for the Mk II MGB at the same time. This neat little selector lever and quadrant was provided on the tunnel.

Rear view of one of the first MGC GTs, showing the only badging evidence the car carried and betraying itself by standing slightly higher off the ground.

made from necessity by giving the car a transverse decorative strip across the front slope of the bulge.

The MGC was quite a lot heavier than the equivalent MGB — 2,460 lb against 2,030 lb being typical figures for new Tourers — and its weight distribution was rather more nose-heavy. Nearly 80 per cent of the extra weight was over the front wheels, which gave the MGC a 55.7/44.3 per cent distribution, compared with 52.5/47.5 per cent for the MGB. Both cars, therefore, were slightly nose-heavy, but the MGC was more so.

The car was announced in October 1967, and was almost immediately available on home and export markets. Unfortunately the cars got a rather lukewarm 'press' (this was at the time when BMC were beginning to struggle and their press relations were in a deep trough — matters improved considerably later); early demonstration cars were not at their best, and the cars released to the technical magazines were little better.

There were two problems — the handling was not nearly as well balanced nor as light as we were used to experiencing on MGBs, with quite a lot more understeer even at optimum tyre-pressure settings, and the engines, though powerful, were not as responsive as the Austin-Healey 3000 units had been.

The result was that the tests published were not kind to the MGC, and it was widely stated that the cars lacked the 'Abingdon touch'. The BMC-modified 2,912cc engines had a lot to answer for, as in standard form they *were* more thirsty, and they *were* much more reluctant to rev. No-one who had witnessed the behaviour of an Abingdon-prepared Austin-Healey 3000 rally car could understand why this should be so, as it was the Coventry Engines Branch which developed those outstanding 210bhp units. The fact was that the redesigned unit had vastly more internal friction and windage losses than the old, and was very little smoother than before. If the Austin 3-litre car had been more of a success (it was not even in production until the summer of 1968, nearly a year after the first MGCs had been built) there might have been justification for engine improvements, but it was not, and both models had to struggle on with what they had.

There was no immediate answer to the handling problem, either, for the extra understeer was due to the increased front-end weight, the heavier steering and the lower gearing (and larger wheel) of the steering itself.

In a straight line, of course, the MGC was a whole lot faster

requirement, and to look after the heavier front-end weight.

There were only minor changes to the rear suspension, but the MGC had Girling instead of Lockheed brakes, larger at the front (11-inch discs) and smaller at the rear (9 x 2½-inch drums). The wheels — disc or optional centre-lock wires as before on the MGB — were of 15-inch diameter with 5-inch rims. This was never justified at the time, and made more puzzling in later years when the next up-engined MGB reverted to 14-inch wheels!

The chassis changes necessitated many new panels under the nose and centre-section of the car; this, together with the changes in the extreme nose to accommodate the forward placing of the radiator, and scuttle/toe-board revisions to accommodate the brake servo and other relocated fittings, meant that the MGC had virtually a new front-end under the familiar skin.

Apart from the larger wheels (which gave the car more ground clearance), and the badging at the rear, the only other obvious difference was to the bonnet. To clear the engine and radiator a wide but not very deep bulge was incorporated, along with a single streamlined bulge to the left side to clear the front carburettor when it rocked under torque reversals. A virtue was

This is the cockpit of an early MGC Tourer, showing that when the revised bodyshell was introduced, along with the modified chassis engineering, it was possible to provide a straight gear-lever (the MGB had had a cranked lever). The lever bezel was entirely different, for the first series of MGBs had had a chrome bezel with recessed bellows. The only way to identify this car as an MGC is (and we cheat here!) by the carburettor bonnet bulge; the two interiors are identical.

than any previous MG road car. Its maximum speed of 120 mph and its ability to sprint to 100 mph in just under half a minute compared well with figures achieved by the last of the Austin-Healeys, but such figures reflect peak-revs breathing capabilities; low-speed torque had suffered considerably. However, if used as a relaxed high-speed tourer it could cover the ground remarkably fast and in great comfort; an MGC GT used in that way was a splendidly civilized machine.

The factory came to terms with the torque deficiencies, but in the time available, and with their own limited resources, they could only improve things by changes to the gearing. From the middle of 1968 the axle ratio on cars with manual transmission was raised numerically to give lower overall gearing and, by definition, more snappy response. Earlier cars could easily be modified like this, as the only changes were to the axle itself and to the speedometer gearing to match this.

All of which was to no avail. The press reports, whether in Britain, Europe or America, were not kind, and the car was

withdrawn from the production lines in August/September 1969 after a run of only two years. A total of 8,999 production cars were built — 4,542 of them Tourers and 4,457 of them GTs. In its only full year — 1968 — the MGC was being built at a rate of about 100 cars a week (compared with 500 MGBs a week). Of the grand total, 3,437 cars stayed at home and 4,256 were exported to North America.

At the end of production, University Motors, MG's largest London outlet, bought the last 176 unsold MGCs, almost all being GTs, modified them — some with very effective Downton engine conversions which improved power, torque and economy, and some with cosmetic improvements — and sold them successfully during 1969 and 1970.

The infuriating thing, as far as MG enthusiasts are concerned, is that all the MGC's problems had a solution, but MG's new masters — British Leyland — would not authorize their introduction. Certainly price was not a problem with the MGC, as it would be with the later MGB GT V8 (in 1969 an MGC GT

On the original (1973 and 1974 model-year) MGB GT V8s, there was a discreet but proud 'V8' badge on the front grille.

Both before and after the soft-bumper style was adopted, the MGB GT V8 carried 'V8' badges on the tailgate.

sold for £1,057 basic price, and the newly announced but very unrefined Capri 3-litre sold for £989 — not a very significant difference), and the performance of the very special works lightweight cars left little to be desired.

When the MGC was dropped, Abingdon returned to building only four-cylinder MGs for another four years, though they continued to mull over ways to produce a worthy successor to the MGC. Even by 1971 they had decided what should be done, but by that time they not only had to convince themselves and their commercial masters at Longbridge, but also the corporate planners of British Leyland in London and elsewhere.

The unsuccessful six-cylinder engine had found no new home after MG had dropped it. The Austin 3-litre car was dropped in 1971 after only 10,000 had been sold (few more than the MGC in more than twice the life), and badge-engined versions of that car were cancelled by British Leyland before they could be introduced. On the other hand, MG were encouraged to look around the Corporation for other suitable engines, the proviso being that they should be capable of relatively easy fitment into the basic MGB bodyshell. Two engines showed promise — the new V-8s being used by Triumph and Rover, respectively.

The Triumph V-8, being fitted in the Stag, was technically more modern, but as MG were still barely speaking to Triumph (as old rivals they could hardly be expected to be friends with them overnight without a lot of soul-searching) it is easy to see why they leaned towards the Rover unit. That engine, in any case, was relatively simple, with a single camshaft and overhead valve gear, it was lighter with aluminium heads and cylinder block, it was larger at 3,528cc, and it was potentially more powerful.

The engineers at Abingdon were also delighted to find that with certain changes to the engine and the structure it was a relatively simple transplant. The new project, therefore, coded EX249 at Abingdon or ADO 75 in overall Austin-Morris language, was gleefully proposed and accepted when it became clear that enough engines could be supplied from Rover's Birmingham factories to satisfy the demand.

The new car, soon given the rather unwieldy name of MGB GT V8, had little in common with the MGC, even though it was really the big-engined successor to this car. For one thing there was never any question of using the MGC's special bodyshell structure and front suspension. Perhaps most important, however, was the fact that it was to be almost entirely a home market model. In the end, only seven cars were ever exported when new, none of them going to the United States.

It was also decided at an early stage that this very fast and silky MG would only be offered as a nicely trimmed GT model. In Britain, at least, there was a very healthy demand for closed sporting cars, particularly up-market models, whereas open-car sales were on the decline. This was a combination of rebellion against the British climate and a general trend towards more civilized motoring.

The reasons for not exporting were several and various. The Rover engine, even though it had been developed from a successful North American design (General Motors had fitted its ancestors to cars between 1960 and 1963), had never been detoxed

to deal with the stringent United States exhaust-emission regulations of the 1970s. Rover had withdrawn from this market in the 1960s, and it was not thought to be economic to carry out such a costly and lengthy development programme for a single MG model. As North America was much the most significant of all MGs export markets this made an attack on other territories unjustified, too.

Even before the new car could be made ready, however, it was upstaged by a private-venture equivalent from Kent, the Costello V-8. The factory's own thoughts stabilized in 1970 and 1971, and at one time they hoped to get production cars announced in 1972, so it is hardly fair to heed the criticism that they looked at Costello's own machine, announced in 1972, before finalizing their own car.

They did not, but a look at the Costello design (made, incidentally, in tiny numbers) is interesting. Compared with the

Powerhouse of the MGB GT V8, built between 1973 and 1976. Unlike the MGC, which it effectively replaced, the V8 used a virtually standard MGB structure and suspensions. However, changes were needed in the engine bay to allow the bulky Rover-manufactured 3,528cc engine to be installed. Because of the line of the bonnet and the height of the engine, the twin SU carburettors were mounted at the tail of the engine, and fed forward into a plenum manifold by secondary cast passages. The air-cleaners were mounted on top of the rocker covers, and they drew air through British Leyland's patented hot/cold air intakes over the exhaust manifolds. Compared with the original MGB (and for the same reason as with the MGC) the radiator had to be mounted further forward and the support diaphragm panels had to be repositioned. Although there was a removable cap on the top tank of the radiator, there was also a remote filler cap and expansion tank on the left side and next to the ignition coil. No attempt was ever made to 'federalize' the V8, and as a result all but seven of the cars built were sold in Great Britain.

definitive Abingdon car it had a different (more powerful) tune of engine, a standard all-synchromesh MGB gearbox, standard MGB GT suspension and special alloy wheels. It was, in every way, a very professionally-executed conversion, marred only by a large but shapely bonnet bulge needed to clear the normal 'Rover' position of the twin SU carburettors. It was also costly (£2,181 basic, £2,443 total — or £2,616 with the 'extras' which would be standard on MG's own car in 1973), compared with the £1,206 basic, £1,459 total asked of an MGB GT in spring 1972.

There was considerable comment in the motoring press when, as soon as Costello's car had been revealed, British Leyland stopped the small-scale supply of V-8 engines which had already been agreed. The fact of the matter is that they did not know the purpose for which the engines had been intended when approving the order, but when they found out they moved swiftly to cut off the possible competition.

Abingdon's own version was delayed due to trivial factors, and was not announced until August 1973. The first production car — chassis number 101 — was built in December 1972 and chassis number 110 in February 1973, but production in series began in April 1973.

Visually the MGB GT V8 — which I will continue to call merely the 'V8' — was obvious from its special alloy wheels (different from those used on the Costello cars), from its badging at front and rear, but most obviously to we British because it sat rather higher off the ground. This was not because of the use of larger wheels — for this car 14-inch wheels were retained, but with 175HR-14 tyres — but because of revised front suspension datum points and differently cambered rear leaf springs. This was done to make the basic structure similar to that which was about to be applied to the MGB, where new North American bumper-height requirements had to be accommodated; for MG this meant that bumpers had to be raised, and in the case of the V8 the difference was one inch.

There was no bonnet bulge on the V8. If the Rover position of the carburettors had been chosen bulges would have been necessary, but the neat MG inlet manifold placed two SU carburettors at the rear of the engine, close to the heater box on the scuttle, from where they fed mixture into the engine through a neat plenum chamber in the centre of the vee. Long forward-facing inlet tracts led from hot-air pick-up points above the twin exhaust manifolds, with air cleaners positioned atop the tappet covers.

The Rover engine, incidentally, was fitted in its 'Range Rover' form, with an 8.25:1 compression ratio (but the Range Rover' of course, used special Zenith-Stromberg carburettors). Although in this form the power output was down to 137bhp (DIN) at 5,000rpm, it could easily cope with all the projected European emission laws, and it still produced a massive 193 lb ft of torque at 2,900rpm, and seemed to pull like a steam engine from very low revs. In every way it looked to have the beating of an MGC, as the magazine road tests soon proved.

The same basic manual gearbox as on the MGB was used (but with overdrive as standard) with yet another set of internal ratios. These must now be listed as follows:
MGB: 1.00, 1.38, 2.17, 3.44, (reverse) 3.09
MGC: 1.00, 1.302, 2.05, 2.98, (reverse) 2.679 (late models)
MGB V8: 1.00, 1.259, 1.974, 3.138, (reverse) 2.819
MGB V8 ratios, like the later MGC's, have not been used on any four-cylinder MGB. Automatic transmission, incidentally, was not available, and had already been withdrawn from the four-cylinder cars due to lack of demand.

Although modifications were needed to the structure of the engine bay to make room for the light but bulky V-8 engine — the inner wheelarches and the bulkhead pressings had to be reshaped — chassis changes were minimal compared with the extensive rework on the MGC. The basic MGB suspension systems were retained, with uprated front and rear springs, but existing four-cylinder-car damper settings and anti-roll bar stiffnesses were carried over.

As on some versions of the MGC, the Salisbury axle's ratio was 3.07:1. This, of course, was linked to the use of overdrive as standard equipment, so in spite of the V8's road wheels being smaller than those of the MGC the overall gearing was even higher. In overdrive, the car wafted along at 28.5 mph/1,000 rpm, which sounded like a sure recipe for really refined and plushy high-speed motoring, and this the car delivered in full measure.

As with the suspension, so with the brakes. The MGC had used radically different brakes compared with the MGB, but the V8 used the MGB's basic system, along with a servo as standard equipment.

Readers will have realised from this summary that the V8 was

The 1975 and 1976 model-year MGB GT V8s looked like this, with the faired-in soft-nose and soft-tail bumpers nicely shaped, but looking too obvious because of their uncompromizing black colour. Like the four-cylinder cars built since this change the V8 was lifted higher off the ground so that USA bumper-height regulations could be met. However, even in 1973 and 1974 form, with chrome bumpers, a V8 always stood that little bit higher, partly due to the larger-section tyres and partly to spring and suspension datum point changes looking ahead to the later laws. The bolt-on cast-alloy road wheels were always a V8 recognition point, and were not offered on other MGBs apart from the 'Anniversary' model. Note the discreet little 'GT' flash on the rear quarter between the side window and the tailgate, a GT feature brought in with the soft-bumper restyle.

really a very desirable car, offering a unique combination of high performance, reasonable economy and a great deal of refinement. No important problems had been encountered in fitting the 3½-litre Rover engine. Why, then, was the V8 car only in production for a little over three years (the last car was made in September 1976), and why were only 2,591 cars built?

There were three principal problems, none of them connected with the technical or functional worth of the car itself. One was that there always seemed to be more important destinations for Rover-produced engines, and MG often found themselves feeling like orphans. The engines were being fitted to the Range Rover and to two Rover saloons — the P5B 3½-litre and the P6B 3500.

(Morgan, too, were taking a handful of engines every week for their Plus-8 model.)

The other reasons were connected with prices — of the car itself and of the petrol and related products needed to run it. No sooner had the car been announced, in August 1973, than the Middle East was plunged into war, and one consequence of this was that the Arab oil producers doubled, then redoubled the price of crude oil as an economic weapon. This meant that any car with a large engine, and which might be expected to use a lot of the precious fluid, suffered a great blow to its prospects. The fact that a properly driven MGB GT V8 could, and often did, record 25 mpg (compared with about 28 mpg for a four-cylinder MGB)

Not quite the real thing! This is one of the rare and very nicely built Costello MGB V8s. Costello started from the basis of a standard MGB V8, shoe-horned in a 3,528cc Rover V8 which retained the original opposed semi-downdraught SU carburettors atop the centre vee (this explains the need for a substantial power bulge in the bonnet panel), and mated this to an MGB Mk II/Mk III all-synchromesh gearbox. The cast-alloy road wheels look similar, but are not the same as those of an Abingdon-built MGB GT V8. The engine, in this guise, was considerably more powerful than that subsequently used by Abingdon and had the 10.5:1 pistons and other details, producing 150 bhp. Performance was electrifying, with a 130 mph top speed and the ability to reach 100 mph from rest in only 22 seconds. It was, however, very expensive at £2,443, a price which did not include overdrive, radial-ply tyres or the alloy wheels, and at the time this compared with £1,570 for a Ford Capri 3000 GT.

made no difference to what prospective customers thought. In their view the V8 had a thirsty 3½-litre engine, and that was an end to it.

The major problem, however, was the car's selling price. It is worth looking at this in simple tabulated form:

1967:   MGB GT £1,094 total   MGC GT £1,249
1973:   MGB GT £1,547 total   MGB GT V8 £2,294

In 1967 the big-engined car had cost 14 per cent more, while in 1973 the premium had rocketed to 48 per cent. We may be sure the V8 engine was by no means as expensive as all that, and we may also be sure that MG themselves would have liked to sell the car at a more reasonable price.

The fault lay with British Leyland themselves, who did not want the V8 to harm Triumph's Stag (£2,533 for the hardtop variety) or even the fast 2½-litre TR6 (£1,653), both of which might have become unsaleable if the V8 had been retailed at a more realistic £1,800 to £1,900. It meant that the V8's prospects

were shackled from the very beginning, and by comparison with the very popular Ford Capri 3000 GXL (£1,824) it looked very expensive. Even the hand-built, but nicely hand-built, Reliant Scimitar GTE could be had for £2,480 with overdrive.

That price tag was a tragedy for the V8, and the sales figures (almost entirely domestic, of course) reflect this. Its best year was 1973, not even a full production year, when 1,069 cars were built, while by 1975 this had fallen to 489 — less than ten cars a week. In 1976, even though the car was not dropped until September, only 176 cars were produced.

By any standards, therefore, the MGB GT V8 *must* have been a commercial disaster to MG and to British Leyland. And yet, throughout its short life, it was always the object of much longing from mere four-cylinder MGB owners, and has now started the steady climb to 'classic car' status. But MG have now learned their lesson; two big-engined MGB exercises have ended in failure, and the experiment is hardly likely to be repeated.

CHAPTER 6

MGBs and MGCs in competition

Works cars 1963 to 1968

Once the MGB had been announced in the autumn of 1962, the company wasted little time in building up competitions versions of the new model. Stuart Turner was now the BMC Competitions Manager at Abingdon, and with the approval of his masters he took a very catholic attitude to the events in which an MGB might shine.

Company policy and sporting regulations were twin problems. The company wanted the cars to be as fast and durable as possible, but also wanted them to be recognizably based on the production cars. The Appendix J regulations, becoming more and more strict as the years rolled by, made it difficult for quantity-production cars to be used in very super-standard condition.

Like the MGA, therefore, the MGB could not be expected to win races or rallies outright. Its forte looked like being as a fast and reliable tool for long-distance races and rallies, where durability would count as much as flashing performance. This did not mean that a properly-prepared MGB would be dull — far from it. In Le Mans guise, with only a lengthened nose to alter the familiar profile, it was capable of up to 140 mph in a straight line.

There was only one exception to the 'build standard cars' rule. In 1967 and 1968, just before the axe fell on the world-famous BMC Competitions Department, two very special MGCs were built and raced with honour. Even in this case, however, the cars' shape was recognizably MGB/MGC; the special fittings were mainly in the form of exotic materials and engine-tuning items.

Abingdon's Competitions Department records are by no means complete for this period of their history, but with their help I have identified 15 separate works cars, each registered locally. Of these, only three had fast-back GT bodies (and two of these were the special lightweight cars).

This preponderance of Tourers is easily explained; they were lighter (and therefore potentially faster) than MGB GTs. In races where high top speeds were possible, good aerodynamics were important, and the Tourers would run with the normal detachable hardtop in position. This item, too, was sometimes fitted for other events where the car could run, rather nebulously but with advantage under the rules, as a Grand Touring car.

Apart from the lightweight MGCs, none of the works cars was specifically built as a racing or rally car. Several machines, indeed, achieved distinction in both branches of the sport. 7 DBL raced at Le Mans in 1963, then won the GT category in the Monte Carlo Rally of 1964 — there can be few greater contrasts than that. Most were raced *and* rallied during their Abingdon careers.

It would be fair to say that very little technical development of the MGB for competition use took place in the six years that the cars were in active use by 'Comps'. A 1963 model was every bit as fast, controllable and reliable as a 1968 model; the exception, once again, was the lightweight MGCs, which had no equivalence with the cars which had gone before (unless it was with big Healeys). There appeared to be little noticeable difference in performance between a three-bearing and a five-bearing MGB engine. Statistical proof of this performance plateau comes from a study of the three different Le Mans cars raced at the Sarthe circuit in 1963, 1964 and 1965. Each car was used in exactly the same visual form (with the Tourer body, with the detachable hardtop in position, and with the unique special lengthened nose

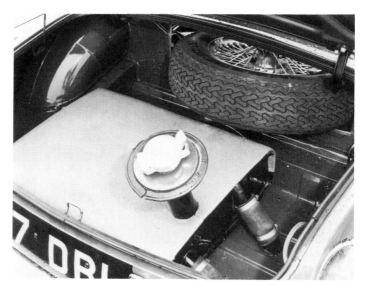

One of the original trio of works competition MGBs — they were registered 6 DBL, 7 DBL and 8 DBL — in race trim, with the bumpers removed, the panelling faired-in and extra driving lights added. The headlamps have their air-smoothing 'Sebring' perspex cowls, the bonnet has a safety strap, and the bonnet release wire is operated by a knob near the left side/flasher lamp. The oil-cooler is visible behind the grille, and circular air inlets duct cold air into the engine bay.

Special competition car items fitted to 7 DBL in 1963. The fuel filler will poke through the boot-lid to the outside world when the lid is closed, and is attached to an auxiliary tank. As can be seen, that tank is then connected to the normal tank by two large-diameter tubes which disappear through the boot floor. The spare wheel (with original-pattern Dunlop SP road/rally tyre) is in a non-standard fixing position, protruding into the passenger compartment.

— which was actually transferred from car to car). Each of the cars — 7 DBL, BMO 541B and DRX 255C — lapped at about 105 mph, and each one could nudge 140 mph in a straight line. There appeared to be no advance in potential during the three-year involvement at Le Mans.

Unlike some other manufacturers in the 1960s, MG made their tuning equipment — engine, transmission and chassis items — freely available, so that private owners could build 'works replica' MGBs of their own. Even in 1978, with the MGB long gone from a place in British Leyland's competition plans, the Special Tuning department at Abingdon still markets a range of special parts. Apart from individual items there are three complete engine kits, the most powerful of which is good for 112 bhp with SU carburettors.

Right from the start, Stuart Turner's department worked the existing regulations to their advantage when preparing competition cars. It was then possible for a manufacturer to specify alternative carburation for his sports cars without having to make more than a nominal quantity available for sale. With the siamesed-port cylinder-head in mind, therefore, MG chose to offer a single sidedraught twin-choke Weber 45DCOE instrument (and an appropriate manifold) in place of the usual SUs.

This, together with a tubular exhaust manifold, was the only visible tuning aid for a works car. Depending on the events entered, more or less razor-edge tuning would be applied, but in 'full-house' racing form the B-Series engine was capable of more than 130 bhp at 6,500rpm — a very creditable 37 per cent improvement on the standard car's output.

It is difficult, however, to be precise about power outputs, as

Detail of a works car's external bonnet-release knob and the fixings for the Sebring-headlamp perspex cowls. These are very early examples of quartz-halogen headlamps, in those days almost worth their weight in gold. Note that there are minor differences between this car and 8 DBL, proving that building works cars is an individual business.

The engine compartment of a racing MGB built at Abingdon. Apart from the fact that this engine has the optional single sidedraught twin-choke Weber carburettor, and there is a fat cold-air duct leading back from the grille to the radiator support panel, it all looks fairly standard.

there were different restrictions for different events. All the engine work was carried out at the Morris Engines Branch factories in Coventry, under the inspired direction of ex-Riley man Eddie Maher; his workshops were also responsible for those magnificently powerful 3-litre Austin-Healey engines.

Most engines were over-bored if regulations allowed this. A standard over-bore of 0.020in resulted in a nominal capacity of 1,821cc, while a 0.040in over-bore gave 1,843cc. It is even possible (with a good cylinder-block) to over-bore by 0.080in — pistons are available from Special Tuning for this — and the resulting capacity is nearly 1,900cc, but this was not allowed for the works cars of the 1960s.

One special engine tune was evolved for 1967 and 1968, and was first seen in 1966 on one of the Sebring cars. With special cylinder-blocks it was possible to bore-out from the standard figure of 80.3mm to no less than 84.7mm, and without altering

the stroke this gave a rather awkward-looking capacity of 2,004cc. Thus equipped an MGB could compete in the 2-litre-to-3-litre 'prototype' class. Though outclassed on performance grounds (power output was about 150bhp at 6,000rpm) it meant that MG could take two bites at the cherry in long-distance events — a ploy which worked well on occasion.

An enormous amount of B-Series engine tuning expertise had been built-up on MGAs and in MG record cars before the MGB appeared. Engines with three-bearing or five-bearing blocks, standard or cross-flow light-alloy cylinder-heads, in racing or in rallying trim, were all familiar, and it is not surprising that the units were usually very reliable. A random failure (like the oil surge and subsequent bearing failures at Sebring in 1963) was a cause for great astonishment, and if the reason became known, for speedy remedial action.

This extra power, of course, was only released by special

A second view of an MGB competition engine bay, this time a car prepared for rallying with the race-tuned Weber-carburettor engine, but with the heater in place and with twin windscreen washer containers. There are also two ignition coils on the inner wheel-arch.

camshafts and with a great deal of attention to cylinder-head shapes and to the porting. Weslake had done the original 1955 MGA Le Mans cars, but when the MGB arrived there was a great build-up of expertise in Morris Engines Branch, with help and boffin-like advice from Daniel Richmond at Downton Engineering in Wiltshire. Special pistons, too, could allow the compression ratio to be raised to at least 11.0:1.

Gearboxes on all the four-cylinder works MGBs (except for the pseudo-MGB, the first 1967 lightweight) were those already developed for the MGAs and Twin-Cams of the late 1950s, with a non-synchronized bottom gear and ultra-close ratios. An innovation compared with the MGAs, however, was that overdrive could be and often was used. Surprisingly, at Le Mans, where one would have thought an overdrive could be really useful, it was never specified, and an ultra-high axle ratio was chosen in its place.

As to axles, the familiar old BMC banjo axle was used at first, but later cars used the much more robust Salisbury-type axle standardized on all cars after the introduction of the GT. A limited-slip differential helped both traction and handling.

In general, the works MGBs were entered for rallies where the car's strength would be an asset and where its handling qualities could make up for any power deficiencies, and for long-distance races like Le Mans and Sebring where the marketing and publicity possibilities were as important as the chances of victory. It is reasonable to say — and absolutely no slur on the MGB's reputation — that the car rarely had a chance of overall victory, but it could and often did perform a giant-killing act which made headlines.

The first three cars — 6 DBL, 7 DBL and 8 DBL — were built at the beginning of 1963, and the first two were sent out to contest the Sebring 12-Hours race. This was now a traditional date for Abingdon's cars, and it also seemed to be traditional that at least one of the cars should be sold immediately after the race and never again figure in Abingdon's plans! 6 DBL, DRX 256C and HBL 129D are all cars which appear only once in Abingdon's records, having been sold in North America after the Sebring race.

That first Sebring race for the MGBs was a real disaster. The first weeks of 1963 in Britain had been arctic in the extreme, and there had been no time to check-out the sump and oil-cooling arrangements which were different from those of the MGA. At Sebring, in the heat of a Florida afternoon, oil surge and hot oil took their toll on the engines, both of which ran their bearings; it was a failure quickly identified, and equally quickly eliminated from future cars.

7 DBL was a busy car in 1963 as it won its class in the sports car race at the Silverstone *Daily Express* meeting, was taken to the Belgian 500 Kilometres race at Spa (Alan Hutcheson being the driver on each occasion), after which it was prepared for the Le Mans 24-Hours race.

For Le Mans the car looked virtually standard, except that it was given a smoothed-out and extended nose in which the air intake was drastically reduced in area, the bumpers removed, and perspex headlamp covers (almost Jaguar E-Type in style) were fitted. Fuel-tank capacity was greatly increased; there were two ways of doing this — by fitting an extra tank in the boot itself, or, where regulations allowed, by fitting a vast 23-gallon tank. At Le Mans the twin-tank solution was chosen, and a very high axle ratio was fitted to allow the car to reach its impressive maximum

7 DBL had a busy life. After competing with honour at Le Mans in 1963 it was crashed in the Tour de France, but then went on to win the Grand Touring category in the 1964 Monte Carlo Rally, driven by the Morley twins, Donald (driving here on the Monaco GP circuit) and Erle. Incidentally, the car was not softly suspended for this event; the roll is a measure of how hard Donald Morley is driving to stay ahead of one of the vast American Ford Falcons, just coming into sight.

By 1966 the MGB was being campaigned in many races and rallies. Here is GRX 307D, one of the most hardworking of all works cars, being thrust through an S-bend on the Mugello road-racing circuit; Andrew Hedges and Robin Widdows shared the driving. The special fuel-filler cap position is clear in this shot, and it is worth noting that the works cars used detachable hardtops wherever regulations encouraged them to run as 'GT' cars.

Unregistered at the moment, this is BMO 541B, prepared for the 1964 Le Mans race, where it was driven by Paddy Hopkirk and Andrew Hedges, performed faultlessly for the entire 24 hours, averaged 99.9 mph and recorded a best lap of 105 mph. Special for Le Mans was the longer nose, which improved the aerodynamics without affecting the engine's performance or the cooling capabilities of the radiator. Three different cars raced at Le Mans in 1963/64/65, but each used the same nose. Other obvious Le Mans fittings on this car are the sockets for the quick-lift jacks (the white 'claws' under the nose), the extra driving lamps, the number-plate illumination, the recognition light on the roof of the hardtop and the roll-cage inside. The slight bulge in the bonnet panel is to give space for the special throttle linkage used with the sidedraught twin-choke Weber carburettor.

BMO 541B showing off the neatly modified rear bodywork, the extra straps to secure the boot-lid and the ingenious way in which the fuel-filler cap for the twin tanks was slotted through the lid. The white brackets under the tail were sockets to receive the quick-lift jacks used by the pit crew.

Inside the boot of the 1964 Le Mans car, with the spare wheel strapped to the top of the auxiliary fuel tank, the special fuel-filler neck alongside it, and the neat mounting of the SU electric fuel-pump. The GB plate is a nice touch — which proves that the car was intended for road use on the continent of Europe!

Compare this pre-1965 Le Mans race-car shot with that of the 1964 Le Mans car opposite. DRX 255C is in almost exactly the same state of preparation. The only differences obvious from the outside are the lack of auxiliary driving lamps (though these were added for the race), the addition of bonnet louvres behind the competition-number roundel, and a marginally smaller radiator air inlet. Oh yes — there is a patriotic Union Jack on the front wing, and the decorative strip on the door has not been painted over!

speed without any danger of over-revving the engine.

It is worth pointing out at this point that up to the end of 1965 the Appendix J regulations allowed lightweight body panels to be fitted 'wherever such panels are licked by the air stream'. On cars like the TR4, for example, where the skin panels were bolt-on items, advantage was taken of this concession, but in the case of the MGB, where all but the doors, bonnet and boot-lid were welded-up to the main structure, it was a very difficult task. A competition MGB, therefore, rarely weighed less than a standard car, and often weighed significantly more due to the extra items carried.

The Le Mans entry was very successful. Even though Alan Hutcheson ran it off into the sand at Mulsanne after only 12 laps (and took 90 minutes to dig it out again!) the car averaged 92 mph for the 24 hours; a quick calculation shows that it was averaging about 99 mph in the 22½ hours it was actually running. It finished 12th overall, its fastest lap was 104.2 mph, and it took second on the 2-litre class behind a very special Porsche. Paddy Hopkirk was the other driver.

Three months later the same car was entered for the 10-day Tour de France, where Andrew Hedges held down fourth overall until he crashed the car on a speed hill-climb.

For 1964, Stuart Turner had more ambitious plans for the MGB, including forays into rallying, and three new cars were built. One — BMO 541B — shone at Le Mans, where in a faultless 24-Hours race it averaged 99.9 mph, lapped at 105 mph and finished 19th overall, driven by Andrew Hedges and Paddy Hopkirk. Later it was used on the last of the classic series of Tours de France, but had to retire.

The outstanding performance of the year was by the Morley twins, Donald and Erle, who took 7 DBL to a serene GT category victory in the Monte Carlo Rally. In the same car, however, they crashed on the Scottish Rally, after which it had to be scrapped.

Two other cars competed in the Liège-Sofia-Liège and RAC rallies, but without success, and it was these experiences which led to a decision to restrict the MGB's main usage to long-distance races.

For 1965 the works fleet was reduced to only three cars — two of them new — and was further reduced to just two cars after the Sebring race in which one car was second in its class. Paddy Hopkirk and Andrew Hedges took 11th place at Le Mans (the MGB's best placing), a class second, and averaged 98.26 mph, which was nearly identical to the result of the 1964 outing.

Another outstanding performance that year was by John Rhodes and Warwick Banks in the two-day Brands Hatch 1000-miles race, when 8 DBL, by now an old campaigner with many thousands of race, rally and practice miles under its feet, won outright.

DRX 255C, pictured on the previous page in long-nose form, was later prepared in standard-shape, and is seen here in race-car trim.

Abingdon only ever built one standard-bodied MGB GT competition car, which was raced at Sebring in 1967, when it won its class, and in the 1968 Targa Florio, where it took second place in its category. The car is seen here, ready for dispatch to Sebring, having been built at Abingdon alongside the all-conquering rallying Mini-Coopers. Apart from the vast fuel-filler cap, in its unfamiliar position behind the right-hand side window, the fitted roll-cage, the strapped-down spare wheel with a racing tyre, and the lack of a rear bumper, it looks remarkably standard.

The works car (entered for obscure policy reasons by Don Moore, the BMC tuning specialist) actually won the first day's 500-mile section, closely followed by Trevor and Anita Taylor in an ex-works car, and outpacing cars like E-Type Jaguars and 4.2-litre Sunbeam Tigers. On the second day the Don Moore car contented itself with fourth place behind a very special Morgan, an E-Type Jaguar and Paddy Hopkirk's works-specification Austin-Healey 3000. The ex-works car had wilted under the strain, and 8 DBL won by a very comfortable eight laps and confirmed that a car does not have to be enormously fast to shine in long-distance events.

For 1966 the sports-car regulations were tightened up considerably, which effectively eliminated machines like the Austin-Healey 3000s and Triumph Spitfires. The MGBs, however, were largely unaffected as they had always been substantially standard, and were to be used even more than before.

Three new cars appeared (one sold immediately after the Sebring race) and new faces in the driving team included the redoubtable Timo Makinen, Julien Vernaeve from Belgium, Alec Poole, and young Roger Enever (Syd's son, who did *not* gain his

The wolf in sheep's clothing — LBL 546E — which was the first of the very special lightweight MGCs. Originally, because it was announced before the MGC had been revealed, it had to race in 'MGB GT' form, and it was like this, as pictured here, that it finished ninth overall in the 1967 Targa Florio. Although the body looked standard, most of the superstructure was of light-alloy, there were wickedly-attractive flared wheel-arches, centre-lock Minilite wheels, and under the skin there was the MGC's new torsion-bar independent front suspension. The car gained its true identity in time for the 1968 Sebring 12-Hours race.

place in the team due to nepotism). Drivers like Makinen and Paddy Hopkirk were ideal team members for the rough and tumble of events like the Targa Florio, though neither, surprisingly enough, were used when the team entered cars in the Marathon de La Route, which was little more than an 84-hour race round the Nurburgring.

Makinen and John Rhodes took GRX 307D to a class win in the Targa Florio, while Andrew Hedges and Robin Widdows repeated this with the same car at Mugello a few weeks later.

Hedges and Vernaeve took the GT category in the Spa 1000-Kilometres race, but the season's outstanding performance was undoubtedly in the 84-hours Marathon.

This event had replaced the Liège-Sofia-Liège rally, which had been hounded off the roads of Eastern Europe by public reaction. The organizers set up an event around the Nurburgring which was almost as much of a race as a rally because it involved continuous high speeds as well as very strict limits on service and refuelling times. It needed great driving endurance and

Two views of MBL 546E as raced at the Nurburgring in the 84-Hour Marathon de la Route, driven by Andrew Hedges, Tony Fall and Julien Vernaeve. After 67 hours it was running strongly in third place, and rapidly catching the leading Porsches, when a miscalculation led to the brake pads becoming worn-out and the backplates welded themselves to the discs; in the end the car finished sixth overall. Since its original state of preparation, the ultra-lightweight MGCs had been given a mesh radiator grille and big air scoops to the front brakes, along with an extra air-intake to the oil-cooler. All except the mesh grille had been added in time for the six-cylinder car to race at Sebring in March 1968. Note that only one windscreen wiper is fitted — there were two on the car as built in 1967. The tail shot shows the tell-tale badging, or rather the lack of badging. When the car was first used with an oversize 2,004cc MGB engine it was badged as an MG GT, and even after the MGC had been announced Abingdon never troubled to fix the correct badges to the car.

application, but also very skilful pit management, which Peter Browning was ideally qualified to provide.

In 1966, therefore, two cars were entered, one being the hard-working GRX 307D, the other an ex-development department hack which had already completed 10,000 miles at 100 mph in a Shell publicity exercise. At the start everything went wrong for MG, for Roger Enever crashed the hack on its first lap and Andrew Hedges crashed the other car on its second lap! Both cars regained the road, that of Hedges/Vernaeve being quite extensively knocked about, and both dragged themselves back through the field. After a sudden thunderstorm which caused the leading Ferrari driven by Lucien Bianchi and De Keyn to crash, the works cars found themselves in first and second positions. After 79 hours, however, the Enever/Poole car broke a half-shaft and had to retire, and it was left to the other machine to take a

splendid first place. In the 84 hours (of which 72 hours were almost continuously spent on the Nurburgring) the car had covered 5,620 miles, and this in spite of Hedges' shunt, after which he had driven round a field for some time trying to find a way out on to the circuit again!

Although a new steel-bodied MGB GT (LBL 591E) was built for 1967 — it raced at Sebring and won its class, driven by Paddy Hopkirk and Andrew Hedges — the rest of the MGB competition story truly belongs to the very special cars coded EX241 to the engineers, and also known as GTS models. These, though based on the design of the MGC already described in Chapter 5, were very carefully built and quite mouth-wateringly interesting to all true MG enthusiasts.

During the winter of 1966-1967 the Competitions Department had gained approval for cars which would be altogether more

One of the two ultra-light GTS cars (as the alloy MGCs were known at Abingdon) being prepared for the 1968 Marathon de La Route. As this car is brand new we may assume that it was RMO 699F, which only raced once under Abingdon's control. This picture reveals that the layout of the structure was absolutely 'standard MGC', and shows the alignment of the longitudinal torsion-bars clearly. Bonnet-release and headlamps-cowling details had not been changed since the first three cars were built in 1963.

A bonnet-full of race-tuned MGC engine in RMO 699F, before it competed in the 1968 Marathon de la Route. This engine, while substantially new, owed much of its racing-development experience to the wonderful old Austin-Healey 3000s used by Abingdon from 1959 to 1965. The big flexible trunking is to channel fresh air into the driving compartment. There was no question of a heating or ventilating kit being fitted. The big transluscent container fixed to the bulkhead is an oil catch-tank.

A very rare shot of the all-aluminium engine fitted to the racing MGCs. Previously, Austin-Healeys had been given aluminium heads, but the light-alloy blocks were new for this project and did great things for the weight-distribution and balance of roadholding. Power output was in the region of 210bhp from this 3-litre engine. Apart from the use of a close-ratio gear-set, and of uprated settings to the overdrive, the transmission was like that of the MGC production cars.

competitive than the virtually-standard MGBs they had been using for four seasons. They also knew full well that the MGC was due to be launched in the autumn of 1967, and they also had a great deal of experience, some of it legendarily successful, with the Austin-Healey 3000s.

The Pressed Steel Company, therefore, produced at Swindon, — at great expense and with a great deal of trouble — six new MGB/MGC GT bodies. These combined a standard pressed-steel underpan with light-alloy skin panels and superstructures, and although the shells looked superficially like those of a standard car, the aggressively flared wheel arches, front and rear, left the onlooker in no doubt of the cars' intentions.

The suspensions were like those of the production MGC, with longitudinal torsion bars at the front, but for the racing application the torsion-bar adjustment could be operated from inside the car, there were extra locating arms to the back axle,

together with a rear anti-roll bar, and all the shock absorbers were adjustable. Light-alloy knock-on wheels were a feature, as were the lack of bumpers and the provision of air scoops to the front brakes, let into the nose. There were four-wheel Girling disc brakes, a fitted roll cage and a 24-gallon fuel tank.

Financial stringency, and the constant rush at Abingdon to keep up with the great success of the rallying Mini-Coopers, meant that only one car was built-up in 1967 (its first race was the Targa Florio in May), and one other was completed in time for the 1968 Marathon de la Route. The other four bodies all found homes in later years, and all but the second race car are known to have survived.

MBL 546E was the first car, and it was first raced as a prototype MGB with the 2,004cc four-cylinder engine first used at Sebring in 1966. In this form (and, incidentally, running with an MG. GT instead of an MGB GT badge on the tail) Paddy

A detail preparation shot of RMO 699F, the second of the very light MGC GT race cars. The location of the special fuel tank, and the enormous filler neck, are obvious, as is the superstructure for the telescopic damper mountings (production cars used lever-arm dampers).

RMO 699F in all its glory, posing after a race-track shakedown run before the 1968 Marathon de la Route.

Hopkirk and Timo Makinen took ninth place, and third in their class, in the Targa Florio.

This car was not used again for a further ten months, when it appeared at Sebring as a true racing MGC. The six-cylinder engines, though related to those of the obsolete big Healeys, were extensively redesigned and less bulky in some respects. All the race/rally knowledge accumulated for the big Healeys could be applied to the new engines, and in cast-iron-block form, with a 0.040in overbore (resulting in a capacity of 2,968cc) the unit produced more than 200 bhp at 6,000rpm, helped by triple double-choke Weber carburettors.

The cylinder-head on this engine was in light-alloy (as it had been on the Healeys since 1962), but on at least one development engine, now sold and fitted to a surviving GTS, an aluminium cylinder-block was also provided. This gave a dramatic weight reduction and made the car's balance even better for circuit racing.

At Sebring the GTS finished tenth overall — the best Sebring place ever achieved by BMC — and it was therefore entered for the 84-hour Marathon de la Route, along with the second car which had been completed during the summer of 1968. According to the form book, such rapid cars, driven by experienced BMC crews, and managed with cunning and flair by Peter Browning's timekeepers, should have been able to win the 1968 event, but unfortunately they didn't make it.

The newest car, driven by Enever, Poole and Clive Baker, retired at an early stage when its engine overheated. The original GTS, driven by Hedges, Vernaeve and Tony Fall, was lying third overall after 67 hours (and at that stage was rapidly catching the leading Porsche 911s), when a miscalculation on brake-pad wear led to the front pads becoming welded to the discs.

Such were the regulations that the car had to be made mobile within 20 minutes or be excluded. The only, desperate, measure was for the car to be sent out *without brakes* — Tony Fall driving — whereupon it completed a Nurburgring lap at an average of 65 mph. Even one more stop could not complete the job in time, and the phlegmatic but cheerful Yorkshireman then went out again, completed another lap two minutes faster than the last, achieved 125 mph on the straights in the brakeless car, and somehow persuaded the engine and transmission to stop him at the pits once again!

This disaster dropped the car by no fewer than 25 penalty laps, and at the end of the event it had dragged itself up to sixth place, 28 laps behind the Porsches. If this was defeat, it was indeed defeat with honour, but the reason for faster-than-predicted brake wear was a mystery to all the mechanics.

This, in fact, was the last official entry of an MG in a motor race, as the department then began to concentrate on saloon cars in rallies to the complete exclusion of motor racing. The two GTS lightweights were prepared for the 1969 Sebring race, but they were entered by British Leyland's North American subsidary. The old firm of Paddy Hopkirk and Andrew Hedges finished 15th in the quicker of the two cars, and this was absolutely the last occasion on which works-prepared MGs and works-paid drivers appeared on a race track.

Factory-prepared competition cars are rarely tried by the motoring press until they have been sold off, so the 'Given the Works' test carried out by Geoffrey Howard and the author in *Autocar* of September 3, 1965, was an almost unique instance. Not only did we have the use of the ex-Le Mans MGB (DRX 255C), straight after the race, with no attention other than a quick oil-change and the fitment of a low (numerically high) back-axle ratio, but we also had the use of an Austin-Healey 3000 works rally car.

Apart from the fact that the silencer had long since lost all its stuffing, and the car therefore made appalling barks and growls as it rushed along, the MGB was in excellent condition. With only the usual pumps to prime the twin-choke Weber carburettor, starting was instantaneous, and even though this was a racing car we were able to use it for commuting and for journeys through heavy London traffic. We found that the suspension was extremely hard, which made the back-end hop about quite a lot, but we also found that the race-tuned engine was really incredibly flexible. Although it wasn't done to pull away from obstructions with less than 2,000 rpm on the clock, pick-up was strong in the middle and higher reaches. Apart from the noise, and the fact that fuel consumption was down to a frightening 14.3 mpg with the 4.55 axle ratio, it was a delightful companion for a hot summer's day.

Even though it was not as special as, for example, a K3 Magnette, this MGB had every characteristic of the Abingdon touch we now know so well.

8DBL led a busy life, and towards the end of its works career it was loaned to John Rhodes and Warwick Banks for the Guards 1,000-miles race held at Brands Hatch in 1965 in two 500-mile sections (on two successive days). It had to run with normal road equipment in place, which explains the presence of bumpers, normal windscreen and the detachable hardtop. Throughout the event, which lasted for more than 13 hours, the car never put a tyre wrong, and eventually won outright, defeating cars like the Austin-Healey 3000 of Paddy Hopkirk and Roger Mac, and several fast Jaguar E-Types, purely on reliability and because it needed far less routine attention at pit stops.

Works competition MGBs and MGCs — 1963 to 1968

1963	MGB	6 DBL 7 DBL 8 DBL
1964	MGB	7 DBL 8 DBL BMO 541B BRX 853B BRX 854B
1965	MGB	8 DBL DRX 255C DRX 256C
1966	MGB	8 DBL DRX 255C GRX 307D HBL 129D JBL 491D
1967	MGB/MGC	DRX 255C GRX 307D LBL 591E(GT) MBL 546E (Lightweight GTS) MBL 547E
1968	MG	LBL 591E (GT) MBL 546E (Lightweight GTS MGC) RMO 699F (Lightweight GTS MGC)

Note: Although six light-alloy GTS bodyshells were built, only two cars were ever assembled. The first car — MBL 546E — raced in 1967 as a 'prototype' MGB — *ie* with a four-cylinder engine in the torsion-bar MGC structure — but became a true lightweight MGC at the beginning of 1968.

Apart from the special wind-cheating noses fitted to the Le Mans cars in 1963/1964/1965, all works cars were raced or rallied in visually standard condition.

One or two other works MGBs were prepared at Abingdon, but are not listed here. This is either:

(a) Because they were used solely as practice cars, or

(b) Because they were immediately delivered to overseas countries for specific events and were never registered in Britain, nor did they ever return to Abingdon.

Overseas readers should note that the last letter in the seven-digit registration mark denotes the year in which the new car was first registered — B denotes a 1964 model, C a 1965, D a 1966, E a January-July 1967 and F a car registered between August 1967 and July 1968. The three original works cars were built at the beginning of 1963.

CHAPTER 7

Prototypes and specials

Including EX234 and ADO 21

How would you have liked the chance to buy one of these MG sports cars designed in the 1950s and 1960s? A monocoque 2 + 2 model, intended to replace both the MGB *and* the Midget, with alternative engines and all-independent suspension with Hydrolastic units? A rebodied MGA with coachwork finalized in Italy, and with a family of V-4 and V-6 engines? Even a mid-engined two-seater wrapped around a choice of tuned Maxi 1750 or E6 2200 power packs, and with De Dion rear suspension?

Of course you would. After all, they were not fantasies, and indeed there were other fascinating projects which never saw the light of day. All these cars ran on the road, and all were partly developed. They were all intended to be built in large numbers at Abingdon. Prototypes of several cars still exist, but are rarely shown to the public.

Although there have really been only five basically different MG sports cars in production since 1945, and only two since 1962, this does not mean that the design departments have been bereft of ideas. Anyone with a feel for the motor industry, and particularly for the Abingdon philosophy, must realise that all manner of things have been proposed from time to time. It is the study of these intriguing 'might have beens' which make an examination of MG's recent history so rewarding.

Nor, in fact, have under-cover MGs always originated at Abingdon. The complex ownership situation, and the often-changed business structure which affected MG's operations, meant that MG projects have popped up from time to time in several places throughout the BMC and British Leyland empires. With so many masters struggling to get their own pet plans approved, it is not surprising that this should be so.

MG, of course, has been a part of the Nuffield Group since 1935, of BMC since 1952, and of British Leyland since 1968. It follows that there have really been three generations of modern MGs, as there have been three of prototypes and specials.

One may ask why none of these interesting cars has ever been produced in quantity, or why they have never been made public after the projects were cancelled. This can be put down to the fact that MG have usually had a very pleasant problem at Abingdon — the public have kept on buying existing models in huge numbers (especially in North America) and still show no tendency to lose interest in them. Other factors, very pertinent for MG, concern mergers, capital spending and other priorities. Whereas a new car to replace the MGB might have looked technically desirable at the end of the 1960s, within the confines of British Leyland a replacement for the Triumph TR6 (now in production as the TR7) was much more urgently needed. With an overall corporate plan *and* the question of investment priorities to be considered, two new cars could not be brought forward together. Nowadays there is a lot more involved in getting approval for a new design than just making sure the design is right!

At this stage, however, I should apologise for having to use a lot of numbers and letters — hieroglyphics, almost — rather than titles for the special cars. Other firms might give their new cars codenames, but at Abingdon they always seem to have had numbers. In the beginning, Cecil Kimber set up a project register, still in use at Abingdon (and making fascinating reading) in which every new car or project was given an EX... (EXperimental) number. Later on, when MG became part of

Once the MGA had become successful there was only one serious attempt to evolve a new body style for this chassis, and this single prototype was the result. In the late-1950s the EX214 project evolved, with a new body styled in concept by the Abingdon design team, but with construction and detail touches by the Italian coachbuilding firm of Frua. As can be seen here they produced an aggressive (some would say vulgar) grille, and there were touches of Maserati in things like the side/indicator lamps. The chassis can be dated as MGA 1500 because it has drum brakes behind the front wire wheels.

The Frua MG, from the tail, showing the neat way in which stop/tail/indicator lamps were faired into the rear wings (they were actually culled from an Italian production car) and the slightly ornate detailing. In the author's opinion this car, suitably Anglicised, would have been as attractive as the MGB project which succeeded it.

The facia layout of the Frua car, EX214, can only be described as an aesthetic disaster, which was altogether typical of Italian styling of the period. While the coachbuilders had a way with sheet metal, they were usually at a loss with interiors, as Fiats and other more expensive sporting cars proved at the time. Details like door handles and window handles are 'Italian coachbuilder specials' and all the facia sheet metal is new, but the instruments and associated switchgear were taken from an MGA 1600, although this model had yet to be announced.

BMC, new cars might also be given overall BMC project codes. An ADO... (Austin Drawing Office, or Amalgamated Drawing Office, depending on who is telling the story) number would be issued from Longbridge, but to confuse matters some cars also carried an EX... number as well, the MGB GT V8 being a good example. It can be bewildering at times, but it is also the only way to pin down the definition of a project accurately.

The special cars which led up to the final design of the production MGA — the George Phillips Le Mans TD, the EX175 prototype and the EX182 racing MGA prototypes — have already been described. From 1952 it was always clear to forward-thinking engineers that a new MG sports car would soon be needed to replace the TD. Syd Enever, who always worked at Abingdon, always wanted it to be the EX175 derivative, but as already recounted Len Lord disagreed with him. The TF, which was no more than a facelifted TD, had to be rushed through as a stop-gap in 1953.

At this time there was still no official MG drawing office at Abingdon. All MG work was controlled by Gerald Palmer, who had personally laid out the MG Magnette/Wolseley 4/44 and the Riley Pathfinder/Wolseley 6/90 saloons (not forgetting his Jowett Javelin design completed at Bradford towards the end of the Second World War); the MG design office was actually only one section of the Nuffield design department at Cowley, where it had been based since 1935. Although it was a very small office under the newly-instituted BMC regime (where the Longbridge design office reigned supreme), engines, gearboxes and axles were all supplied as major components to be worked into what remained of the Nuffield influence.

At the time there was lengthy discussion, much of it heated, about the next MGs. Some characters wanted to retain the traditional styling while others wanted to leap boldly to the type of car which Syd Enever was proposing. Palmer and his merry men, with a shrewd eye to company politics, therefore proposed the best of both worlds; they suggested a new car which could have both styles of body without vast tooling expense!

This ingenious project, conceived in 1953 at Cowley, could have been based on the existing TF chassis (this model was just about to be introduced), and would have retained the Nuffield XPAG/XPEG engine and transmission. Careful design of the steel bodyshell (not at all obvious from the only official studio pictures which survive) meant that it could have been built with traditional flowing wings and tail, or with more up-to-date full-width styling in the latest fashion, all by the use of bolt-on skin panels and new doors.

In this way a new MG model could have been marketed with two different body styles, perhaps simultaneously in the same markets, and customers would have made up their own mind which they wanted. Although at the time Gerald Palmer thought that the balance might tip in favour of the traditional design, he was soon to change his mind and agree that a modern MG style was what was needed. This project never got very far.

Chronologically, the next under-cover MG development after the MGA had been readied for its launch in 1955 was the construction of the first twin-cam engines. Palmer's part in the Twin-Cam which eventually reached production in 1958 has already been mentioned in Chapter 2. In 1954-55, however, it had a rival, designed by Bill Appleby at Longbridge (he had been involved with Murray Jamieson in the design of the fabulous 750cc Austin twin-cams of the 1930s); as already related, the

Morris unit was first raced in the 1955 Tourist Trophy.

It was Len Lord's policy at BMC to encourage inter-factory rivalries, and there was no tight cost control to ensure that duplication of effort was avoided. In the case of the two twin-cam engines Lord no doubt was influenced against the original Gerald Palmer/Morris Engines Branch design merely because it had been born in Oxford. The Appleby engine, designed at Longbridge and therefore under his personal control (Lord was a compulsive 'designer' as well as a chief executive!) was therefore a favoured design.

However, it was the Morris Engines design which went on to power the Twin-Cam, in much modified form, and the Longbridge engine was dropped. The reasons for this were purely economic, for both engines produced about the same power output and both were strong and potentially reliable. The Morris Engines version, however, had much in common with the existing B-Series production design, which was already used in the MGA and many other BMC bread-and-butter cars, while the Longbridge design was entirely special. Not even Len Lord would sanction capital for an engine which had few other obvious applications, so it was cancelled.

At this stage it is worth noting that Gerald Palmer designed a twin-cam conversion for the 2.6-litre six-cylinder C-Series engine, which was the engine powering the big Austin-Healeys from 1956 onwards. He intended it, originally, as a unit to make a Jaguar-beater out of the Riley Pathfinder and to replace the old 2,443cc Riley 'Big Four'. The Morris Engines Branch completed detail design, and one engine was built (it looked much like the MGA Twin-Cam's engine, as one would expect), but only one car was run at Abingdon, and the same economic considerations killed it off. Such an engine, if it had gone ahead, would have been a

This is the original wind-tunnel model produced at Abingdon for a very specialized racing MGA, once projected for 1956. It was coded EX186, had a prototype Twin-Cam engine and De Dion rear suspension allied to a normal MGA-type chassis-frame. The bodyshell would be of light alloy, and the driver sat behind a wrap-round screen with a headrest behind his head. One car was actually built to this specification (although pictures no longer exist), but after the events of 1955 BMC forbade MG to go racing in 1956, and it was sold off to an enthusiast in North America.

A trio of quarter-scale wind-tunnel models produced at Abingdon when the car to succeed the MGA was being evolved. From left to right these are: EX214, the Frua shape, this time with a fast-back hardtop proposal; EX205/1, which was an early MGB proposal based more closely on the EX181 record-car nose than was later thought to be desirable; and EX205/2, which was another step on the way to finalizing the proper MGB Tourer body shape.

EX205/1 in more detail. This style was proposed in 1958-1959 for a monocoque car to replace the MGA, and although it was soon thought to be too big and bulbous, and to have too long a wheelbase, it is apparent that MG had a pretty clear idea of the way they wanted sports-car shapes to evolve. This should also convince doubters that it was MG, and not Pininfarina, who evolved fastback coupe shapes for their MGB sports car. At this stage, however, there was no thought of having a large and so-useful tailgate/loading door; this prototype merely had a conventional boot-lid. This mock-up, incidentally, is full-size, but is built of wood and clay (the windows, for instance, are quite opaque), and it was never destined to become a running prototype. The windscreen was deeply curved, like that of the MGA Coupe. The MGB GT, of course, was to have very little curvature in its screen.

'natural' for assessment in the MGCs of the 1960s.

With the MGA in production, Abingdon's design team had time to look around for improvements and additional projects. The MGA Coupe followed (and of course the Ted Lund Le Mans car was an ultimate development of that shape), along with the still-born EX186 Le Mans car with its special low-drag body and De Dion rear suspension.

Record cars like EX179 and EX181, together with the ADO 13 sports-car project (which became the Austin-Healey Sprite on announcement in 1958), kept Abingdon very busy later in the 1950s. EX181, however, with its wind-tunnel-designed shape, was a great influence on the body stylists, who began to think of ways to smooth-out their production cars. This influence, of course, affected the development of the MGB, but before this there were two attempts — one major and one minor — to rebody the MGA.

The minor effort was to apply a forward-leaning type of nose to the MGA shell — in effect grafting an MGB style of nose on to the existing shell — but this would have involved sheet-metal changes to bonnet, bonnet surrounds, nose panels and inner structural panels. In any case, the new and rather higher nose did not really match the unchanged swept-down tail.

The major effort was more serious, and involved a completely new bodyshell on the existing MGA chassis frame. Christened EX214, this started life with Don Hayter's team at Abingdon as a series of body skin lines, which were then supplied to Frua in

Italy. Frua were requested to build-up one complete prototype to this style and to design a suitable interior for it.

The decision to use Frua instead of Pininfarina was strange, as Pininfarina were already contracted to BMC for such work (the Austin A40 of 1958 was the first public indication of their collaboration with BMC), but the reason seems to have disappeared in the mists of time. At the end of the 1950s, however, BMC's top management at Longbridge were convinced that Italian coachbuilding was the best, and they were often prepared to spend money to have schemes built-up into full-scale prototypes, rather than study small-scale models or sketches.

Frua built just one prototype on a wire-wheeled MGA chassis, in open form. In many ways, as the illustrations confirm, this car had touches in common with the Ferrari and Maseratis of the day. This, of course, was inevitable; not only were Don Hayter and his team influenced artistically by what Italy was doing, but Frua were also constantly involved in building special bodies for motor shows.

I have to say, with hindsight, that I find EX214 a rather flashy creation, with one or two touches which surely would have been toned down before it reached the production lines. The general shape, with its clever notch ahead of and above the rear-wheel arch to signify a separate rear wing shape, is fine, but front side-lamps, over-riders and particularly the grille are not in the MG tradition. The screen, too, had considerable wrap-round, which the MGA had not (and neither would the MGB).

BMC management must have thought the same, for after it had been hawked around the decision-makers at Abingdon and Longbridge it was firmly rejected. Shortly after this the body was cut-up and the MGB project got under way. Even so, there was still time for a quarter-scale model of an EX214 fast-back coupe to be built and tested. This model still exists at Abingdon, along with several other legendary shapes evolved in the 1950s and 1960s. Together with the fast-back Le Mans MGA, this proves that MG designers were thinking along the basic lines of a GT MG long before the MGB GT took shape in 1964.

Occasionally it was thought that the MGA should have a more sophisticated rear-suspension location. Both a coil-spring-and-radius-arm system (retaining the live axle) and an all-independent system were proposed, but neither progressed very far. On the other hand, at the beginning of the 1960s there were intriguing possibilities of a new family of BMC-designed engines.

Alec Issigonis was pursuing a design policy of very compact saloon-car layouts, and vee-formation engines loomed large in his master plan. When the Morris 1100 was announced in 1962, with acres of spare space all around the puny A-series engine, Issigonis when asked for the reason, smiled enigmatically and murmured: 'Wait and see!'.

We waited, and never saw, but for many months BMC were involved in a new engine series. Later, of course, it was Ford who took up this theme, but it was definitely BMC who first embraced the thought of a V-4 and V-6 engine family using standardized tooling. The angle between cylinder banks was 60 degrees, with a single central camshaft; valve operation was by the very complex BMW/Bristol type, which included cross pushrods and part-spherical combustion chambers.

For the MGA, and subsequently for prototype MGBs, a 2-litre V-4 engine was proposed. In the MGA this dropped into place fairly easily, although it was surprisingly wide; the bonnet opening, however, was a restriction on access, for although long it was surprisingly narrow. To be practical for production purposes an enlarged bonnet panel would have been needed.

The V-6 version, in 3-litre form, was also proposed for early versions of ADO 51/ADO 52 (which eventually became the MGC model) but almost before any serious work could be done the entire project was cancelled. This, incidentally, explains why there was a rush of new engines from BMC in the 1950s — A-Series in 1951, B-Series as a modified Austin engine in 1954, and C-Series also in 1954 — then no other new engine until the Maxi unit of 1969. Cancellation was for several economic and political reasons involving BMC's hierarchy, and was not at all regretted at Abingdon. The V-4 unit was proving a pig to balance properly (Ford found this with their Capri V-4 units in the 1960s and 1970s), and both engines would have been heavy and expensive. Number-freaks will want to know that the V-4 MGA was EX216.

Apart from finalizing the MGB GT body, the development history of which has already been detailed, and designing a fast-back coupe top on an MGB for possible use at Le Mans in 1965, the designers then took a back seat and concentrated on the MGC.

In the meantime, by the end of 1966 or beginning of 1967, thoughts were turned seriously towards a successor for the MGB. This, remember, was in the 1960s, when all the sports-car manufacturers thought prosperity was going to be a continuous business, that the Americans were not serious in their mouthings on safety and exhaust-emission limitations, and that a car should be replaced well before it was over its peak. If they started now, they reasoned, a new car would not be ready before the end of 1969, by which time the MGB would have been in production for seven years; the MGA, after all, had lived for just that period.

At first they thought of modifying the MGB by giving it an independent rear suspension, but this necessitated a subframe, which in turn would mean wholesale changes to the bodyshell, and Pressed Steel would ask a small fortune to do the work. Oh hell, someone thought, we might as well do a completely new car anyway!

EX234, therefore, began to evolve in 1967. Logically it would have been the MGD if it had been produced, but it was altogether more important even than this — it was also intended to replace the Midget! At the very least, if BMC had not considered this practical, it could have plugged the wide gap between the 1,275cc Sprite/Midget and the 1,798cc MG sports car. Ford of Detroit had refined the idea of offering several engines in one bodyshell to a great degree and introduced the concept to Britain with the Capri of 1969. MG, to their credit, had been thinking along similar lines since the mid-1960s.

EX234 was to be no larger than the MGB, and because in one version it could have been powered by the BMC 1,275cc engine it

The beautifully shaped EX234, the rationalized sports car which MG wanted to replace the MGB at the end of the 1960s. It was styled by MG, but constructed by Pininfarina in 1968. As conceived it could have replaced both the MGB and the Midget, for it could have used either the 1,275cc or the 1,798cc engine. It had an 87-inch wheelbase (the MGB wheelbase is 91 inches), had all-independent suspension links and Hydrolastic suspension units. This, the only prototype, had 13-inch wheels, but the 1,275cc car would have used 12-inch wheels.

The superbly finished interior of the EX234 prototype, showing that it was so well packaged as to provide a very genuine 2 + 2 seating arrangement. The facia and tunnel-console layout was almost too good to be true (MGBs, at the time, were not in the same class), yet it was all designed to be built in large quantities. What would it have been called? Well, both MGB and MGC were in production, so logically it would have become the MGD . . .

This is how the small-engined version of EX234, really a Midget replacement, could have looked, without any brightwork or decoration. The door-release button and grip were as neat as could possibly be. The hood would probably not have looked like this in mass-production form. This car was not rejected because of any technical defects, but because of the burden MG were having to face with rationalization into British Leyland, and the onset of time-consuming North American safety and exhaust-emission regulations. Capitol Hill has much to answer for!

This 1968 picture shows off the really delicate detailing of EX234. It is not eulogizing too much to suggest that it required no changes before being committed to production, except for the conveniences of mass production. Those are MGB side/flashing indicator lamps. It is interesting to note that this side of the car was decorated with a horizontal flash which terminated at the door-release mechanism, while the other side of the car (for viewing as the small-engined type) was plain.

A small number of specially-modified MGBs were produced by Jacques Coune, the Brussels coachbuilder, called the MGB Berlinette 1800. They were substantially different from the Tourer in many ways, with the front wing/headlamp arrangement being modified, an entirely new windscreen and coupe top being fitted, and wind-up window alterations being made in the doors. There was a pronounced spoiler on the tail panel. This car, however, was not the inspiration for an MGB GT, thoughts on which had been maturing for a long time before this special car appeared in 1964.

had to be as light as possible. Further, there was to be 2 + 2 seating (MG's sales staff already knew that the MGB GT was being criticized for not having occasional rear seats), all to be squeezed into a monocoque pressed-steel structure of about MGB bulk.

There was to be a choice of engines and transmissions — basically these would have been the Sprite/Midget and MGB units — and there would have been all-independent suspension. Corporate policy made sure that Hydrolastic suspension, interconnected front to rear by small-diameter pipes but without self-levelling, would be incorporated. A wishbone front linkage and a semi-trailing rear linkage were chosen. Wheels would have been 12-in (with the small engine) or 13-in diameter, and the whole was based on an 87-in wheelbase, which was four inches less than that of the MGB.

Apart from the Hydrolastic suspension and the front and rear layouts, the only major mechanical novelty was the chassis-mounted differential. In isolation this would have been quite an expensive item for which to tool up, but fortunately the BMC empire had all manner of strange items in use. In this case, the differential casing was that used at both the front and the rear of the Austin Gipsy four-wheel-drive cross-country vehicle, which had all-independent suspension of its own. The Gipsy had been in production since 1958 (though it would be phased-out at the end of 1967 while EX234 development was proceeding), and the differential used standard B-Series components from the same family as those of the MGB. The Gipsy's ratio, however, would have been useless for EX234 — it was 5.125:1!

Abingdon built-up one prototype as a structural rolling chassis, then shipped it off to Pininfarina, who completed a very attractive prototype and sent it back to Abingdon for assessment.

It was an instant success, and a study of the pictures will show why this was so. Even though there was much more space in the passenger compartment (back-seat passengers would, however, have been drastically short of leg room, as usual), and even though the nose was much stubbier than that of the MGB (there would be no chance of accommodating a lengthy six-cylinder engine in this car), it was a remarkably pleasing shape, which stands the acid test of viewing from almost every angle.

There were definite family resemblances to Sprite/Midget and MGB cars (the prototype even used MGB side/indicator lights at the front), and apart from considerations of production convenience there was virtually nothing which needed changing. Only one open prototype was built, though Pininfarina already knew how they wished to treat the layout of a GT model. The prototype had a lush and sumptiously trimmed interior and facia, which might have had to be simplified to meet BMC cost targets, but was otherwise very attractice.

All in all, EX234 was a brilliantly conceived and integrated concept, of which Cecil Kimber and his MG innovators would surely have been proud. The Hydrolastic suspension raised little enthusiasm at Abingdon (team driver Timo Makinen once tried a Hydrolastic Midget, and his comments are quite unprintable here), but in the face of corporate instructions nothing could be done at that early stage. Even the Mini-Cooper S cars, after all, were being built with Hydrolastic suspension, though Stuart Turner's works rally cars were regularly run to the old obsolete 'rubber' specification. Hydrolastic, I should point out, rapidly lost favour after new engineers arrived at Longbridge to begin the post-Leyland rationalization, and eventually was to be found only on the long-running Austin Maxi model.

Yet for all its brilliance EX234 was abandoned in 1968. For MG people this was a disaster, a real heart-breaking decision, even though the commercial reasons for it soon became clear. The problem was that the full impact of the new North American safety and exhaust-emission legislation was just beginning to weigh hard on the MG design staff. Their total engineering strength was always tiny — it rarely reached 50 in the 1960s, of whom no more than 15 to 20 were designers — and the hard fact was that they could either go ahead with the development of a major new model and all its variants, or they could make sure that existing Midgets and MGBs could be kept in the market in North America.

At the time EX234 was merely shelved, as everybody hoped that they would soon be able to take it out again, dust off the neglect and re-awaken their ideas, and make the car a production proposition. But that day never arrived. For years EX234 was given its own private little corner at Abingdon (it was kept snug and dry, but well away from prying eyes), and it was not until 1977 when, still in remarkably good condition and still painted in 'EX181 green', it was sold off to that arch-collector of all good MGs, Syd Beer.

In the meantime, too, Leyland and BMC having merged, every member-company's product policies were thrown back into the melting pot. MG, for instance, were instructed to take another look at the existing MGB, and at one time were asked to instal the Maxi E4 1,750cc engine — in its rare in-line form — in case the venerable B-Series unit was to be phased-out.

It was from the top echelons of British Leyland, indeed, that the most intriguing of all MG projects came along in 1969 and 1970. For some time there had been deep (and in MG's view

heretical) thoughts about the future for BLMC's various sports cars. This led to what was to all intents and purposes an unofficial design competition — Triumph were asked to make proposals for a new front-engined car (this, of course, matured in 1975 as the TR7) while MG were commissioned to look into a new mid-engined concept!

This, incidentally, meant that Abingdon had been involved in all three basic layouts in the 1960s. They knew all about the conventional, or 'classic' layout from their own production cars and they had seriously investigated front-wheel-drive for the A-Series Mini-based Sprite/Midget projects, ADO34 and ADO35, at the beginning of the decade.

When I was first told about this exciting mid-engined machine I was not even allowed to look at the schemes and sketches which resulted, but now I am very happy to be able to publish hitherto-secret views of the new car, coded ADO 21 in Longbridge language, as its shape was finalized in the Longbridge styling department (which is always known irreverently as the 'Elephant House') in November 1970. The style had nothing in common with anything which Pininfarina or Michelotti might have proposed. It was purely and simply a Longbridge creation, from the department then controlled by Harris Mann.

It was a wickedly attractive car, with a very sharp wedge nose, pop-up headlamps, a small near-vertical back window and two spins from the rear of the doors to the tail. There was enough shaping in the various sections to make it sensuously beautiful, with none of the sharp-edged planes which characterize other mid-engined machines of the period. It may help to put it in perspective by reminding ourselves that Mann's stylists were finalizing the dumpy little Allegros at about the same time, would next turn their attention to the TR7, and soon afterwards would produce the wedge-shaped Princess models. I have absolutely no doubt that in refined and productionized form it would have been a sensation.

ADO 21, though styled at Longbridge, was completely engineered at Abingdon, and would effectively have replaced the MGB and the MGC. It was built-up around the transversely-positioned Austin Maxi 1750HL engine and gearbox, though space was also schemed around it for the closely-related six-cylinder E6 engine of 2.2-litres or even 2.6-litres to be installed. This meant that in Maxi 1750HL form the car would have been

The special-bodied Pininfarina Austin-Healey 3000, first shown in 1962, undoubtedly had some influence on MG's body engineers when they were planning the MGB GT. The 'greenhouse' is altogether too similar to that of the MGB GT for the two cars to have evolved completely separately from each other. This Austin-Healey design was styled by three young men for an *Automobile Year* competition at the 1962 Geneva Show, and their prize was to have Pininfarina construct a car to their designs. Their names, for posterity, were Pio Manzu', Michael Conrad, and Henner Werner. Abingdon certainly saw this machine before the end of 1962 (the factory was building Austin-Healey 3000s, of course in those days), but the MGB GT was not finally shaped until 1964.

behind the engine, in the tail. With North American safety requirements particularly in mind, siting the petrol tank was a real headache, solved finally by keeping it away from all the crash barriers by slotting it in between the seats and the engine.

It was another splendidly integrated design, which matched EX234 in its sheer practicality and potential saleability, but it was yet another of the MG projects to be cancelled. The only car built, a converted MGB, was not preserved and has been cut-up. Only the drawings and the photographs remain.

A great deal else of an experimental nature has happened at Abingdon over the years, but some of the schemes border on the bizarre and some were purely one-offs. Apart from the multifarious Sprite/Midget schemes, which included one car built with the MGB engine (and raced, incidentally, by Syd Enever's

son Roger), there have been saloon and coupe ideas which have little relevance to the sports cars being described here.

The most significant in the MGB's final years, of course, was the proposal to re-engine it with a 1,993cc overhead-cam O-Series unit (which had been revealed in 1978 and subsequently fitted to the Princess, Marina and Ital models). In twin-carb form for the UK, something like 110bhp (DIN) would easily have been available, while for the USA it ought to have been possible to get the power up from the 65bhp of the latter-day B-Series MGBs to at least 80bhp or more. This engine, incidentally, would have been mated with the Rover-Triumph five-speed gearbox (TR7-type) and possibly with the TR7's rear axle. Prototypes had been built by 1978, but the cost of legal homologation for the USA versions would have been horrendous and the project came to nothing.

CHAPTER 8

Buying and older MGA, MGB or MGC

What to look for, restoration and the 'Best Buys'

This chapter is intended as a condensed guide for the millions of sports car enthusiasts who always wanted an MG, but somehow never got round to buying one. In the limited space available I hope to show that some MGs are better than others, that low-production variants can be very desirable today, and that some particular versions (especially of the MGB) are not as nice as others.

But I must make it quite clear that I cannot dig deep into the detail problems which develop in the various modern MGs as they grow older, nor can I do more than sketch the restoration methods you might apply to a neglected car.

Of course there is an enormous choice. Getting on for 600,000 MGAs, MGBs and their derivatives have now been made, and a large proportion of them survive. Well over half of these cars were sold originally in North America, but until very recently MGBs were being exported to almost every country in the western world. The cars have been around for so many years that there should be a good choice near you.

One thing which always worries me is that some cars take on a cult value, and the prices at which they change hands soar away from any reasonable level. I'm very much afraid that good versions of the MGA are already involved in this process, despite the fact that so many were built, and it is a fact that a 1962 MGA 1600 Mk II, for instance, will probably sell for a lot more than a 1963 MGB.

To get a feel for the number of cars around I ought to summarize the production figures of each model. These are:

			To USA
MGA 1500	1955-1959	58,750	48,431
MGA 1600 Mk I	1959-1961	31,501	25,219
MGA 1600 Mk II	1961-1962	8,719	6,468
MGA Twin-Cam	1958-1960	2,111	1,035
MGB Tourer Mk I	1962-1967	115,898	71,722
MGB GT Mk I	1965-1967	21,835	10,160
MGB Tourer Mk II/III	1967-1980	271,777	228,552
MGB GT II/III	1967-1980	103,762	37,161
MGC Tourer	1967-1969	4,542	2,483
MGC GT	1967-1969	4,457	1,773
MGB GT V8	1973-1976	2,591	7

The figures are correct up to the end of production in 1980. For Abingdon-assembled cars the delivery figures can be further summarized as follows:

All MGAs: Home 5,815; USA 81,153; elsewhere 10,394
4-cyl MGBs: Home 115,336; USA 347,595; elsewhere 50,341
MGC/MGB V8: Home 6,021; USA 4,263; elsewhere 1,306

There are discrepancies between these totals and the overall figures for cars produced quoted elsewhere in the book, the difference being explained by the practice of sending CKD cars in packs to various countries for local assembly.

I have nearly finished with basic statistics, but I think it is worth drawing attention to the following breakdown of MGB GT deliveries:

MGB GTs built 125,597. To Britain 65,322; to the USA 47,321. This proves that the Americans have been much more addicted to open-air motoring than we British, who are understandably so much more cautious about our weather! Incidentally, the MGB GT was withdrawn from the American market at the end of 1974, or that figure of 47,321 would undoubtedly be higher by now.

The first fact which becomes abundantly clear is that the supply of MGAs in Britain is very limited indeed, which might begin to explain why their 'classic' or hoarding values are currently going through the roof. There should, of course, be a very much wider choice in some export territories, notably the United States.

The figures also bring home the fact that neither the MGC nor the MGB GT V8 sold very fast. Paradoxically, although this infers that neither car was very popular when it was a current model it also means that supplies are now rather limited, and for this reason alone a considerable demand has been built-up for them both.

What is surprising is that these big-engined MGs sold much better, relatively speaking, at home than abroad. The rarest MGs of all in North America, of course, are MGB GT V8s, of which only seven were delivered when new. It is possible, however, that a few more have slipped in through the back door since then.

So which are the Best Buys, and are there any cars to be avoided? Does the fact that a particular car did not sell well mean that it was a poor example of its type? On the other hand, does a best-seller really deserve the raving success it had? The answers are rarely simple.

Let us consider, first of all, the rarer variants of the two breeds; the MGA Twin-Cam, the MGC and the MGB GT V8 all have their rabidly-enthusiastic following, and all have become something of cult cars.

By the end of the century, no doubt, the Twin-Cam will have become a nearly mythical beast in MG folklore. Only 2,111 were built and sold, and despite the fact that their present-day owners invariably treat them with great respect, stocks of spare cylinder-heads are now exhausted, and Leyland are no longer supplying any part of the car which is different from the pushrod-engined 1500s and 1600s from the same period.

The Twin-Cam did not sell fast, but it was nevertheless a splendid car. The problem was that it required more intelligence and finesse of its owners, and a great deal more care and attention

from its dealers, than it usually received. There was nothing amiss with chassis, brakes, or roadholding. All the problems came from the engine, and these can be summarized as an unhealthy thirst for oil and a finicky need for the highest quality fuel. Poor fuel (and particularly incorrectly-set ignition timing) led rapidly to piston-burning.

The cars which have survived are the ones given low-compression pistons (all BMC Gold Seal rebuilds have these, as did the last batch of production units) and iron piston rings. These, between them, cured the engine's bad habits, and any such surviving MGA Twin-Cam is prized and loved by its owner. The Coupe version is exceptionally rare.

The 1600 De Luxe (Mks I *and* II, in spite of what some historians suggest) were really 'homologation specials', and as stated, only 395 of them were ever built. They inherited everything from a Twin-Cam, brakes and all, except for the engine. This makes them the best of all the pushrod MGAs, and that is saying quite a lot!

Now to that most controversial of all modern MGs, the MGC. This car, when new, had an almost universally bad reception by the motoring press. Nowadays, however, the MGCs which remain appear to be in great demand, and there is a body of people who insist that they are better cars than the later MGB GT V8s; this, of course, is a matter of opinion, and is not a sentiment shared by this writer.

Owners and devotees of the MGC, however, have come to terms with its little ways. Just so long as you do not expect an MGC to handle with the same precision and spirit as an MGB, nor expect it to out-perform the V 8-engined cars, it could be the car for you. But in standard form it *is* a bit ponderous, and it *is* a heavy understeerer. This does not make it an unworthy car, but unfortunately it has had to stand comparison with the older Austin-Healey 3000 which effectively it replaced, and it did not have quite the same character.

There is no doubt, however, that the University Motors versions of the MGC, with either their Stage I (150 bhp) or Stage II (175 bhp) engine, are altogether more exciting. Not only are the engines more powerful, but they are (or should be) perfectly balanced and therefore much more silky, and have really lusty low-speed torque. They have more luxury equipment than a normal MGC, but the handling is virtually unchanged. The 130

CHAPTER 9

Spares and maintenance

Including the clubs

If you own and love an older car, even if it is a renowned 'classic', you must come to terms with the fact that spares and technical assistance may be hard to find at the factory. Even though MGs come from a factory with a famous name, and have fine reputations, spares-supply problems certainly exist.

The basic problem is one of passing years. The oldest MGA, by now, is approaching its 27th birthday, and even the youngest 1600 Mk II was built more than 20 years ago. Since the Leyland Cars spares division at Cowley has a policy to support an obsolete car for 10 years after it goes out of production it is easy to see that the spares stock of MGA items is very thin indeed. The MGB, being a current model in much-modified form, is better served, but even so the earlier models with their three-bearing engines and allied details are beginning to suffer.

Leyland, in fact, recognize the fact that a much greater proportion of MG sports cars are preserved for great periods than bread-and-butter saloons would be, and make their spares provisioning calculations on that basis, but there are limits beyond which they are not prepared to go.

However, the good news is that in Britain, in the United States and elsewhere there are specialist MG clubs dedicated to the preservation of their cars, their maintenance and their restoration to original glories. If the factory decides to let a particular part go out of stock, the clubs are often able to step in and have those parts manufactured.

First a word about Leyland's policy and methods. All MG spare-parts stocks are now held in the vast building at Cowley, on the eastern edge of the old Morris-Pressed Steel complex. MG, at Abingdon, hold no stocks of spares, nor have they done so since the late-1950s, when BMC rationalization began to intensify. At Abingdon, in fact, there is now no spares or service facility of any nature. All queries — and this includes technical and specifications requests — are handled at Cowley, where there is a staff which specializes in MG matters.

Cowley is the functional and warehousing centre for MG spare parts. Even though there are many more MGs in North America than there are in Britain, Cowley still holds many more spares than the Leyland importing centre at Leonia, and supplies huge quantities of parts on a regular basis. They claim to be able to supply 95 per cent of current-model parts immediately against a dealer's or distributor's stock order. The other statistic which brought me up short when I asked for information was that Cowley holds more than 60,000 different MG parts (sports cars and others), of which about 10 per cent provides 90 per cent of the turnover.

There is no hard-and-fast rule about obsolete stocks, as to which will be remanufactured or which will be allowed to die gracefully. Although the policy of supporting a car for 10 years after it has gone out of production is stated, many parts or components are bought on a 'one-order-for-life' basis at the outset of this period. On past experience, Leyland claim, they can judge the demand for things as diverse as a wing panel or a king-pin, a steering wheel or an instrument, a damper or an over-bore piston. But if demand for a part is still steady and predictable when stocks begin to run dry, consideration is always given to having further new parts made.

The problem is always an economic one. Cowley admit that they do not have body panels remade unless the press tools and dies can be stocked economically in the interim period, and they also claim to be in the hands (and subject to the policies) of outside suppliers for things like electrical items and instruments.

For all modern MGs one spares advantage is that there is a great deal of commonization of major components like engines and transmissions with other Leyland (Austin-Morris) models. The MGA/MGB four-cylinder engines, for instance, are all in the B-Series family which, though likely to become obsolete by the end of the 1970s, has been used in virtually every type of vehicle from a family saloon to a light van, in transversely-mounted front-wheel-drive or in-line installations, from the 1950s to date. Although many MG parts are unique to these sports cars, the general demand for B-Series parts of all ages is such that service support is guaranteed for a long time to come.

Although the all-synchromesh MGB gearbox is not now fitted to any other vehicle in the Leyland range except the Sherpa van it is still a current-production item and therefore in good supply. The old B-Series gearbox, though not used in MGBs built after the end of 1967, is still serviced due to the demand for parts from the wide range of cars and vans which used in-line versions of the B-Series engine. Even the gear-wheels themselves, of MGAs and early MGBs, are sometimes the same as those used in other models.

The same remarks apply to rear axles. The later Salisbury-type axle (recognized by having a central differential housing casting and welded-in half-shaft tubes) is a current production unit; there is no spares supply problem, particularly as the axle ratios have never been altered. The earlier B-Series axle (recognized by its banjo-style casing) used on all MGAs and on MGBs up to 1967 (but never on the GT) is also still serviced because of its wide use in other BMC models. It is worth noting, however, that the axle ratios involved (4.3, 4.1, and 3.909) were by no means as ubiquitous; in particular the 3.909 ratio appears only to have been used for MGBs and supplies of that item are inevitably becoming scarce.

Leyland make the very valid and whimsical point that holding stocks of complete replacement bodyshells is an expensive way of storing fresh air, and that for this and other reasons they rarely hold on to shells for more than two or three years after a car has been withdrawn from the market. British readers will know that from time to time the company sells-off obsolete shells at bargain prices, though the writer cannot recall this ever having been done for an MG sports car.

There are absolutely no stocks of MGA bodyshells, and while Leyland do have MGB monocoques they reminded us that these are now confined to the latest models which have the big black bumpers; surely no MG enthusiast needs to be reminded again that behind those big bumpers there is a great deal of difference, making late model shells difficult to adapt to early specifications?

It may be hard for enthusiasts and restorers to accept, but Leyland's opinion is that if a bodyshell or a monocoque is so badly bent as to need renewal then that car should, however reluctantly, be written-off. They apply the same philosophy to MGA chassis frames, which are no longer available, but this enormously robust item must be very difficult to neglect badly enough to suffer from terminal corrosion, so *unless* an MGA is crashed badly it should never need a frame.

Conversation with MG specialists at Cowley reveals that the stocking situation regarding individual parts is complex. Some parts sell regularly and are often reordered for the vast warehouse, while other parts have been dribbling on for many years (sometimes selling more slowly than was originally forecast) and will not be supported once the bin is empty. They make no secret, however, of the fact that if one part goes out of stock, there is often a viable alternative from some other Leyland (Austin-Morris) model, and that people are employed at Cowley with just the sort of specialist knowledge to be able to suggest these alternative sources if a customer is desperate.

This is not to say that an MG owner should contact Cowley direct. The only approved way of ordering spares is through an MG dealer or distributor, and if you find that such people are not really very interested in looking after older models you should make sure that you order a part by its Part No. — and keep nagging. There *are* customer-relations people at Cowley who like to think that their customers are kept happy; I have to say that most cases of a customer having difficulty in getting spares can be traced to the reluctance of his dealer to take the trouble to research precisely what he wants.

The fastest-moving items are trim parts and body sheet-metal. Trim can usually be made by specialists, even if the factory have abandoned the particular part (with diligence, even the original type and colour of material can usually be traced), and this is one area where a factory does not agonize too much about holding stocks (the permutations, in any case, are enormous).

Sheet-metal parts for MGAs and MGBs are held for as long as reasonably possible, but the sheer lack of space means that Pressed Steel have had to abandon their dies for the MGA models, and stocks of parts are no longer available. For the MGB, even for early models, there is no problem, but Cowley make the point that in certain cases the panels are stocked in non-pierced condition, so that the different badges, chrome lines and other model-year details can be added after delivery.

Some MGC parts — mechanical and sheet-metal — are still stocked, but I know that a great many of the slow-moving but major items have now become impossible to find. This is because only about 9,000 cars were made, and it follows that spares for the rare MGB GT V8 are bound to disappear even quicker. But Cowley's expertise is such that they soon identified the transmission troubles being suffered by this model and then made suitable spares provision for it.

One of the necessary aids to preservation and especially restoration of MG sports cars is to know exactly what goes into a car. Apart from the car's instruction manual, which should be in every car from the day it is delivered, it is surely a good thing to get hold of an official Workshop Manual and especially to link this with a Parts Book.

As with mechanical spares, a stock of these books — from MGA to date — has been maintained until demand has dropped right away. The bad news is that several of these manuals are no longer available from the factory, but this is not an ultimate tragedy. In Britain, and in the United States, at least (and probably in other countries, too) the company has granted republication rights to specialist MG clubs and individuals on the understanding that none of the recommendations are altered or otherwise bowdlerized.

But in strictly commercial terms we cannot expect dealers to be very interested in MGs which are long since obsolete. So how should you cope?

This is where the clubs can be so useful. There are MG clubs in most countries where there are MGs, and while some of them concentrate on motor sport and the social side of things, others are mainly (and commendably) concerned in the preservation and maintenance of all historic models.

This section must, therefore, start with the MG Car Club Ltd., the original MG club, set-up as long ago as 1930, with John Thornley as its original organizing secretary. Thornley soon joined MG, and apart from his factory duties he continued to support the club in every way he could. The company gave financial support, membership rose rapidly, and factory staff had to be taken on to deal with its administration. Wilson McComb (the distinguished MG historian) joined the company in 1959 as the club's general secretary, and started the magazine *Safety Fast* which is still the official organ of the club.

Following the formation of British Leyland in 1968, financial support for the club was withdrawn and the Abingdon office had to be closed. Lengthy negotiations by the club's officers led to the title (and this is where the 'Limited' suffix came in) and the *Safety Fast* magazine being taken on. The club has been completely independent since 1969.

The MG Car Club caters for all types of MG, of all ages, and membership is not confined to MG owners. At the last count there were more than 5,000 British members and more than 8,000 members in the various overseas sections. Both figures are growing. The club's activities are mostly competitive (sprints, hill-climbs, trials, driving tests, gymkhanas) and social, and more than 1,000 events of all types take place every year.

The club's links are worldwide. *Safety Fast,* which is free to members, lists nine British Centres, 26 North American Centres, along with branches in most European countries, Japan, Canada, Australasia (four in Australia, one in New Zealand) and Africa.

In Britain there are eight registers, each of which caters for separate model groups. As far as this book is concerned, MGAs, MGA Twin-Cams and MGCs are covered — there are no MGB facilities yet because this is still a current model.

Now, here are the addresses. Leader of the orchestra, as it were is:

Gordon Cobban, General Secretary, MG Club Ltd., P.O. Box 126, Brentwood, Essex CM15 8RP.

Registration and membership are looked after by:

Syd Beer, The MG Museum, St. Ives Road, Houghton, Huntington, Cambridgeshire.

There really isn't space for me to list all the contacts worldwide, but if you were to join the club and begin to receive *Safety Fast* you would find the addresses listed on a regular basis.

From time to time the club is offered the chance to buy obsolete spares which Cowley is clearing out, and a new company — CK Spares Ltd. — has now been formed to look into the manufacture of new spares from original factory blueprints and has been licenced officially by British Leyland to undertake this. At the time of writing, however, they are not yet ready to tackle the manufacture of new body panels.

Various MG specialists, incidentally, advertise in *Safety Fast*, and the club's officers point out that if they were not of the highest integrity they would not be allowed to use these pages to promote their businesses. All manner of spares and services are provided, which makes the magazine a useful directory to what is available.

As far as historical records are concerned, although MG have kept no details about models previous to the MGB (for which they still hold precise chassis-build records right back to the first production cars of summer 1962), the MG Car Club can help in many ways, and anyone considering authentic restoration should get in touch with them.

In Britain, at least, there is one great rival to the original club, which has to be measured as a great success because it has built a membership of 5,000 in only five years. This is the MG Owners' Club, based on the little village of Over, in Cambridgeshire, which caters specifically for owners of later MGs, notably MGAs, MGBs, MGCs and the Sprite/Midget family.

Unlike the original club, the MG Owners' Club placed its emphasis on parts location and supply, technical advice and assistance, and more recently on the renewed publication of certain vital documents like Workshop Manuals and Parts Lists.

The General Secretary is:
Roche Bentley, The MG Owners Club, 13 Church End,
Over, Cambridgeshire, CB4 5NH.

Roche assured me that the Owners' Club is in no way in competition with the Car Club, and that their aims and ambitions are entirely different. Many MG owners, he pointed out, are members of both clubs.

With the emphasis on restoration and maintenance there are spares secretaries for each type of car, and the permanently staffed headquarters at Over have a good supply of technical literature which can be duplicated and supplied at a suitable price. The club magazine, *Enjoying MG*, was enlarged greatly in 1975 and now contains regular features about the technical and restoration aspects of more recent MGs.

The Owners' Club has excellent trade links, and members can often buy parts and accessories at discount prices. Of equal importance is that the club has a list of recommended suppliers, regularly and ruthlessly updated. They have also appointed a club insurance broker to specialize in sports car problems and particularly to arrive at realistic values for cars which have already taken on a more valuable 'classic' status.

Finally, I think I should repeat my step-by-step advice for any MG owner needing parts and not knowing how to find them:

a) First try to establish the actual part number of the component you need. To do this you may need a Parts List, which may be difficult to find in a hurry — unless, that is, you are a member of one of the clubs already noted above. But *in every case* it is essential to know the Chassis No. of your own car, and be able to quote it to any firm or individual ready to supply your needs.

b) Armed with the number, see if your MG dealer can supply, or can be persuaded to try to supply it. If he is an accredited MG dealer and uses their microfilm display machine properly he should soon be able to tell you if the item you want is still normally stocked by Leyland at Cowley.

Is he reluctant to get involved? Then persist. If you get no satisfaction, then contact the Customer Relations department at Cowley and give them all the facts. But remember that parts cannot be supplied direct to you from Cowley; they will have to be supplied through a dealer.

c) In any case, you should be a member of one of the clubs in your country or area. Not only will they provide companionship, but they will also be able to offer advice, succour and probably point you in the direction of specialist parts suppliers.

In the end, however, please remember that the pleasure of owning an MG sports car should really be concentrated in driving it rather than in just looking at it, unless, that is, you are a Concours nut, in which case you will possibly never use your pride and joy from one event to the next. Happily, an MGA, MGB or MGC has a splendid name for reliability, for spirit and for sheer long life. That is why so very many cars, well past their first flush of youth, are still in daily use all round the world. They gave great pleasure when new, and in this increasingly conformist world they probably give even greater pleasure today.

Although the last MGBs rolled off the production line in October 1980, the launch of the Limited Edition (LE) models was delayed by BL until January 1981. There were just 1,000 of these cars, 420 of them being open Tourers in metallic bronze with gold 'LE' side livery and 580 being GTs in metallic pewter with silver side livery. Centre-lock wire-spoke wheels were fitted to 208 of the open cars, while all the others had cast-alloy wheels and 185/70SR-14in tyres. The last two cars of all — a Tourer and a GT — went into the care of BL Heritage.

APPENDIX B

Chassis number sequences — by model and year

Model	Years built	Variant	Chassis Nos.
MGA 1500	Aug 1955-May 1959	1,489cc	HD10101-68850
MGA 1500 Coupe	Oct 1956-May 1959	1,489cc	HM20671-68850
MGA 1600	May 1959-Spring 1961	1,588cc	G/HN 68851-100351
MGA 1600 Coupe	May 1959-Spring 1961	1,588cc	G/HD ''
MGA 1600 Mk II	Spring 1961-July 1962	1,622cc	G/HN2 100352-109070
MGA 1600 Mk II Coupe	Spring 1961-July 1962	1,622c	G/HD2 ''
MGA Twin-Cam	Spring 1958-Spring 1960	1,588cc	YM1, 2, 3 or 5 501-2611
MGA Twin-Cam Coupe	Spring 1958-Spring 1960		YD1, 2, 3 or 5 501-2611
MGB	July 1962-Oct 1964	3-bearing engine	G/HN3 101-48765
MGB	Oct 1964-Oct 1967	5-bearing engine	G/HN3 48766-138799
MGB GT	Oct 1965-Oct 1967		G/HD3 71933-139823
MGB Mk II	Oct 1967-Oct 1969	all-synchro box, etc	G/HN4 138800-187210
MGB GT Mk II	Oct 1967-Oct 1969	all-synchro box, etc	G/HD4 139284-187210
MGB 1970 model-year	Oct 1969-Aug 1970		G/HN5 187211-218651
MGB 1971 model-year	Aug 1970-May 1971		G/HD5 219000-256646
MGB 1972 model-year	May 1971-Aug 1972		258001-294250 and 294951-294987

Model	Years built	Variant	Chassis Nos.
MGB 1973 model-year	Aug 1972-Sept 1973		294251-294950 and 295301-327990
MGB 1974 model-year	Sept 1973-Sept 1974		328101-360069
MGB 1974½ model-year	Sept 1974-Dec 1974	soft-nose	360301-367818
MGB 1975 model-year	Dec 1974-Sept 1975		367901-386267
MGB 1976 model-year	Sept 1975-June 1976		386601-409400
MGB 1977 model-year	June 1976-Sept 1977	suspension and interior changes	410001-444499
MGB 1978 model-year	September 1977 onwards		447001 onwards
Final Chassis Numbers	Autumn 1980	Tourer GT	523001 523002

Chassis Number definitions for MGBs

Typical Chassis Number is: G/HN5 U 234567 B

1st prefix letter	G = Marque name, MG
2nd prefix letter	H = Engine type, 1,400 to 1,999cc in BMC line-up
3rd prefix letter	N = 2-seater Tourer body
	D = Grand Touring Coupe body
4th prefix number	3, 4 or 5 = Model series
5th prefix letter	U = United States market (no prefix for other markets)
6th prefix letter	A, B, C, etc = Model-year built. A denotes 1970 model-year and J is for 1978 model-year. This notation was introduced from the start of 1970 model-year production.

MGC	July 1967-August 1969	G/CN	
		101-9099	
MGC GT	July 1967-Sept 1969	G/CD	
		110-9102	
MGB GT V8	April 1973-Sept 1976	G/D2D1-	
		101-2903	

Notes: There have been only three distinctly different sequences of Chassis Numbers for four-cylinder cars built since 1955 — for the push-rod ohv MGAs, the Twin-Cam MGAs and for the MGBs. There were separate sequences for the MGCs and the MGB GT V8s.

In the case of MGAs one series led directly to another. In the case of MGBs, however, there are certain minor gaps; cars of a certain model-year may have been discontinued at a random Chassis Number, but Chassis Numbers for the *next* model-year usually start from the next convenient round figure.

Model-year production is by no means the same as calendar-year production; this is to allow early models to be shipped out to the United States in time for the beginning of a calendar-year's sales.

Other cars built at Abingdon — 1955 to 1980 inclusive

While the MGA, MGB and MGC ranges have been in production large quantities of other models have been built on parallel assembly lines at Abingdon. These were:

Make and model	Years built	Quantity produced
MG Magnette ZA/ZB	1953-1958	36,600
MG Midget 948cc	1961-1962	16,080
MG Midget 1,098cc	1962-1966	36,202
MG Midget 1,275cc	1966-1974	100,345**
MG Midget 1,493cc	1974-1979	73,899
Austin-Healey 100/6	1957-1959	8,391
Austin-Healey 3000	1959-1968	42,924
Austin-Healey Sprite 948cc	1958-1962	69,449
Austin-Healey Sprite 1,098cc	1962-1966	37,120
Austin-Healey Sprite 1,275cc	1966-1971***	22,793
Riley Pathfinder	1954-1957	5,152
Riley 2.6 saloon	1957	434
Riley 1.5 saloon	1957	150
Morris Minor Traveller	1960-1964	10,867
Morris Minor van	1960-1963	9,147
Vanden Plas Princess 1500/1750	1979-1980	1,217

**Between January and March 1967 a total of 476 Midgets and 489 Sprites were assembled at the BMC Cowley works.

***The Sprites built in 1971 were known as Austin Sprites (the Healey name was deleted), carried a chassis prefix A/AN10, and comprised 1,022 cars.

APPENDIX C
MG production and deliveries — 1955 to date

The detailed charts included in this Appendix show — year on year, model by model, for home, export and in particular for the USA — the way in which MGA, MGB and MGC sports cars have been built and sold between 1955 and the end of 1977. The MGB, of course, continues in large-scale production.

I should emphasize one thing. Production figures are by calendar year and not by any parent company's financial year, which means that production is counted from January 1 to December 31. This will explain the considerable discrepancies between, for example, a 1972 production figure and the inference of a 1972 model-year output. Cars built for a particular model-year would probably start in September/October of the previous year and run out 12 months later; this is to allow for the delivery 'pipeline' effect for cars to be shipped to the USA and other export territories.

There are also minor discrepancies between cars actually built and the numbers which could be inferred from a study of the appropriate Chassis Number sequences. This is explained by one or two minor gaps which occur at important model changeovers, and where it was thought 'tidy' to start again from a round figure.

The production chart shows some interesting details:
(a) That a few old-model Mk I MGBs were built in the first days of 1968, even though the Mk II version had been announced in October 1967.
(b) That the first three MGB GT V8s were built at the end of 1972, even though the model was not actually launched until August 1973.
(c) That production of the MGA Twin-Cam had virtually ceased by the end of 1959, even though it was listed well into 1960.
(d) That 1961 and 1962 were very poor years for the MGA model, which is partly explained by the fact that the MG Midget was being introduced in 1961 and production of the MGA ceased in July 1962.
(e) That production figures for the MGB Mk II are carried on up to date, even though the car has been known unofficially as a Mark III in some quarters since the autumn of 1971. At Abingdon, in fact, the car is more accurately defined nowadays by its model-year specification with respect to the all-important USA market.
(f) That the half-millionth MGB was built at Abingdon shortly before the end of the 1979 calendar year.

TOTAL DELIVERIES

Model	Home	Export — USA	Export — other	Total***
MGA 1500	2,687	48,431	5,722	58,750
MGA Twin-Cam	360	1,035	583	2,111
MGA 1600	2,172	25,219	2,658	31,501
MGA 1600 Mk II	596	6,468	1,431	8,719
MGB Tourer (Original)	19,420	71,722	18,720	115,898
MGB GT (Original)	8,034	10,160	3,433	21,835
MGB Tourer (Mk II)	30,594	228,552	12,631	271,777
MGB GT (Mk II)	57,288	37,161	9,313	103,762
MGC Tourer	1,403	2,483	656	4,542
MGC GT	2,034	1,773	650	4,457
**MGB GT V8	2,584	None	7	2,591

**Note: Because the V8 engine was never cleared for emission-limited operation the MGB GT V8 was never exported to the United States.

***Note: Totals for MGA and MGB include CKD kits.

MGA/MGB/MGC Production figures — 1955 to date

Year	MGA 1500	MGA Twin-Cam	MGA 1600	MGA 1600 Mk II	MGB Tourer Mk I	MGB GT Mk I	MGB Tourer Mk II	MGB GT Mk II	MGC Tourer	MGC GT	MGB GT V8
1955	1003										
1956	13410										
1957	20571										
1958	16122	541									
1959	7644	1519	14156								
1960		51	16930								
1961			415	5670							
1962			3049	4518							
1963				23308							
1964				26542							
1965				24179	524						
1966				22675	10241						
1967				14568	11067	560	329	189	41		
1968				108	3	17247	8349	2566	2462		
1969						18896	12134	1787	1954		
1970						23866	12704				
1971						22511	12169				
1972						26222	13171				3
1973						19546	10208				1069
1974						19713	9638				854
1975						19967	4609				489
1976						25860	3698				176
1977						24482	4198				
1978						22006	5658				
1979						19897	3473				
1980						11004	3424				

APPENDIX D

How fast? How economical? How heavy?

As far as performance is concerned, I do not believe in quoting from factory handouts. Nor, for that matter, do I trust the enthusiastic figures quoted by some of the fringe magazines. The figures tabled here are reliable. They have been recorded by independent and authoritative motoring magazines from test cars loaned to them by MG in England, or by the North American subsidiary company.

All British-specification cars are as tested by *Autocar,* while all the 'federal' figures are those recorded by *Road and Track* in the United States. I have not troubled to list *Road and Track* figures for pre-1966 models, as these were unaffected by exhaust-emission engine control and would have been mechanically identical with home-market cars.

In terms of bare figures, the 'federal' tests tell a depressing story. Since 1966 the MGB has suffered a persistent and progressive strangulation to its engine output, and its weight has tended to creep up.

Conversely, the performance of a British-specification MGB has barely altered in the 15 years that the car has been in production. *Autocar's* first MGB test was published in October 1962, and its latest Tourer test was conducted in April 1975. Comparative acceleration figures were usually within tenths of a second of each other, the maximum speed was up by 2 mph due to the use of overdrive (though the speed in direct top gear was up by only 1 mph) but — creditably — the car's fuel consumption was much improved (from 21.4 to 26.1 mpg) in the later car.

Purely for interest — because they refer to a Le Mans works MGB fitted with an ultra-low 'rallying' 4.55:1 axle ratio — the last set of figures show the get-up-and-go which a properly tuned and prepared car can give. The car in question had completed 24 hours in the 1965 Le Mans race, was merely given a service and an axle change, and given to *Autocar* for their 'Given the Works' series. It may not be standard — but 0-60mph in 8.2 seconds, 0-100mph in 25.0 seconds and a standing quarter-mile sprint in 16.3 seconds is quite an eye-opener. That car, incidentally, was used by *Autocar* on the road for more than a week, and exhibited no temperament of any nature. The car's maximum speed, of course, was limited only by engine revs (6,500 rpm) and with its proper Le Mans gearing it could achieve about 140mph.

	MGA	MGA Coupe	MGA 1600	MGA 1600 Mk II	MGA Twin-Cam	MGB	MGB	MGB GT	MGB	MGB GT	MGB GT	MGB
	1,489cc	1,489cc	1,588cc	1,622cc	1,588cc	1,798cc	1,798cc o/d	1,798cc o/d	1,798cc Auto	1,798cc o/d	1,798cc o/d	1,798cc o/d
Mean maximum speed (mph)	98	100	101	101	113	103	103*	101	104	102*	105*	99
Acceleration (sec)												
0-30mph	4.9	4.7	4.6	4.4	4.3	4.1	4.0	4.0	4.9	3.8	3.5	4.8
0-40mph	—	—	6.7	6.8	6.9	6.2	6.0	6.2	7.1	6.1	5.5	7.0
0-50mph	11.0	10.8	10.3	9.7	9.4	8.5	9.0	9.3	10.0	8.7	8.2	9.3
0-60mph	15.6	15.0	14.2	13.7	13.3	12.2	12.9	13.6	13.6	13.0	12.1	14.0
0-70mph	21.4	20.1	18.5	18.1	17.3	16.5	17.2	19.0	18.5	17.8	16.5	19.1
0-80mph	32.1	29.1	26.6	24.6	22.5	22.9	24.1	25.4	26.4	25.4	22.7	28.5
0-90mph	50.1	45.2	36.4	36.1	30.0	32.6	35.6	38.1	39.0	36.9	34.5	35.7
0-100mph	—	—	—	—	41.1	52.3	—	—	—	—	—	—
0-110mph	—	—	—	—	—	—	—	—	—	—	—	—
Standing ¼-mile (sec)	20.2	19.3	19.3	19.1	18.6	18.7	18.9	19.1	19.5	18.5	18.3	19.1
Direct top gear (sec)												
10-30mph	—	—	—	—	—	—	—	—	—	—	—	12.5
20-40mph	12.2	12.7	11.0	12.7	11.0	11.4	8.6	11.1	—	11.2	10.8	11.5
30-50mph	12.3	12.0	10.9	11.6	10.2	9.7	8.7	10.8	—	10.1	9.5	9.9
40-60mph	13.1	12.2	10.5	12.0	10.5	8.7	9.1	10.8	—	9.6	9.3	10.9
50-70mph	15.0	13.7	11.9	12.7	11.7	10.4	11.1	12.6	—	10.8	10.9	16.9
60-80mph	18.1	16.6	13.2	13.9	11.7	12.0	13.2	15.3	14.5	13.7	12.6	22.2
70-90mph	—	—	17.0	18.2	13.6	15.7	17.1	20.4	19.4	19.0	17.0	32.0
80-100mph	—	—	—	—	18.7	29.8	—	—	—	—	—	—
90-110mph	—	—	—	—	—	—	—	—	—	—	—	—
Overall fuel consumption (mpg)	27.0	28.0	24.1	22.3	21.8	21.4	22.0	22.8	25.5	23.7	26.1	25.7
Typical fuel consumption (mpg)	30	30	27	27	25	25	27	26	26	24	28	28
Kerb weight (lb)	1,904	2,107	2,030	2,016	2,156	2,072	2,128	2,379	2,144	2,379	2,289	2,442
Original test published	1955	1957	1959	1961	1958	1962	1965	1966	1970	1971	1975	1977

*In overdrive top.

	MGB GT 1,798cc	MGB 1,798cc	MGB 1,798cc	MGB GT 1,798cc o/d	MGB 1,798cc	MGB GT 1,798cc	MGB 1,798cc	MGC 2,912cc o/d	MGC GT 2,912cc Auto	MGC (Federal) 2,912cc o/d	MGB GT V8 3,528cc o/d	MGB Le Mans 1,821cc
				——— Federal specification ———								
Mean maximum speed (mph)	105	104	104	105	94	96	90	120	116	118	124	105
Acceleration (sec)												
0-30mph	4.0	3.9	—	—	4.6	5.0	5.5	4.0	4.4	3.7	2.8	3.2
0-40mph	6.3	6.0	—	—	6.9	7.5	—	5.6	6.2	5.4	4.3	4.6
0-50mph	9.9	8.4	—	—	10.0	10.7	—	7.6	8.2	7.2	6.4	6.6
0-60mph	13.6	12.1	12.1	13.6	13.7	14.6	18.3	10.0	10.9	10.1	8.6	8.2
0-70mph	18.3	16.7	—	—	19.0	20.2	26.5	13.8	14.6	13.6	11.8	11.8
0-80mph	25.1	23.2	—	—	27.5	29.5	39.0	18.0	18.8	17.8	15.1	14.8
0-90mph	37.2	32.8	32.8	—	—	—	—	23.1	26.3	—	19.0	19.2
0-100mph	—	—	—	—	—	—	—	29.3	35.8	32.6	25.3	25.0
0-110mph	—	—	—	—	—	—	—	40.9	—	—	35.6	—
Standing ¼-mile (sec)	19.6	18.7	18.7	19.6	19.2	20.2	21.5	17.7	18.2	18.0	16.4	16.3
Direct top gear (sec)		— Top-gear acceleration figures not recorded by ROAD & TRACK										
10-30mph								11.1	—	—	7.5	—
20-40mph								9.6	6.9	—	6.8	—
30-50mph								9.1	8.1	—	6.5	—
40-60mph								10.0	9.6	—	6.6	6.2
50-70mph								10.7	10.7	—	6.8	6.3
60-80mph								11.1	11.7	—	7.4	6.2
70-90mph								12.8	13.9	—	8.3	6.9
80-100mph								15.4	16.4	—	10.3	11.8
90-110mph								18.3	—	—	14.8	—
Overall fuel consumption (mpg)	28.75	30.0	29.4	24.1	—	—	24.4	17.5	19.0	22.25	23.4	14.3
Typical fuel consumption (mpg)	—	—	—	—	—	—	—	19	20	—	25	—
Kerb weight (lb)	2,308	2,220	2,220	2,345	2,250	2,380	2,275	2,477	2,615	2,600	2,387	—
Original test published	1966	1968	1970	1971	1973	1973	1976	1967	1968	1969	1973	1965